Mama 'n 'Nem

HANDPRINTS ON MY LIFE

Greta Oglesby

Kirk House Publishers
Minneapolis, Minnesota

Mama 'n Nem
Handprints on My Life
by Greta Oglesby

Cover photo by Drew Flynn.

Library of Congress Cataloging-in-Publication Data

Ogelsby, Greta.
  Mama 'n nem : handprints on my life / Greta Ogelsby.
    p. cm.
  ISBN-13: 978-1-933794-48-8 (alk. paper)
  ISBN-10: 1-933794-48-8 (alk. paper)
  1. Ogelsby, Greta. 2. Ogelsby, Greta—Family. 3. Actors—United States—Biography. 4. African American actors—Biography. I. Title.
  PN2287.O32A3 2012
  792.02'8092--dc23
  [B]
                              2011048794

Kirk House Publishers, PO Box 390750, Minneapolis, MN 55439
www.kirkhouse.com
Manufactured in the United States of America

DEDICATION

This book is dedicated to my mother, who was simply the most gracious woman I've ever known and the best friend I could ever have, who exampled for me what it is to live a grace-filled life. Her compassion for people, and her genuine love and humility continues to leave an indelible impression on my heart and my life. Thank you, Mama, for the countless precious memories, for instilling in me a strong sense of self-worth, and for pointing me towards my own personal truths.

To my husband, Dennis, the love of my life and my biggest fan: I am the woman I am today because you've allowed me not only to grow, but also to flourish in my own individuality within our oneness. Only a man with an enormous heart and an extraordinary sense of self can embrace the true harmony in that. Honey, thank you so, so much. I love you madly.

To Meghann and Chase, my rhythm and blues: God gave you both to me, two shining examples of his amazing grace. I'm so proud to be your mom.

Special thanks to
Sandye & Gary Moore

CONTENTS

FOREWORD

The people presented on these pages are aunts and uncles, cousins, grandparents, neighbors, and of course Mama and Daddy. The accumulation of their years and wisdom has largely shaped who I am today. They were my lifeblood, my cocoon, my inspiration. They were my guardians, my heroes and sheroes who left a legacy that continues to inform and define my life.

For the past fifteen years or so, at every family gathering, we'd find ourselves sitting around a dinner table sharing family stories—poignant, counterfeit, true, rich, and hilarious stories, stories that always begin with "Remember the time when . . ." And someone would always exclaim: "Somebody should write this stuff down!"

My brother Shane recently bought a house in Las Vegas. We thought it only fitting to christen his new home with life, laughter, food, and fellowship. The very first night we sat around his dining table and howled with laughter until the wee hours of the morning. I love our times together, just sitting around sharing stories. It has become a ritual for us, and we look forward to those times when we as a family gather together and share stories old and new, with Daddy our patriarch leading the repartee.

On the plane ride back home, "Somebody should write this stuff down" kept reverberating in my head. So I began to write, and the words effortlessly began to flow. My hope is that readers will find *Mama 'n Nem* inspiring, rich, and full of life.

These elder women taught me sisterhood and gave my life resonance; collectively they were the embodiment of everything I wanted to be in a woman. But the familial umbrella I sit under stretches wide. They were cooks and hairdressers, preachers and teachers, housekeepers and painters, maids and army men. Navigating through the hardships of day to day living, they constantly fought the age-old battle of life and liberty with the pursuit of happiness. Each of them gave me something significant and intangible. They endowed me with gifts of the soul: dignity, respect, grace, passion, spirituality, a positive self-image, humor, simplicity, and sincerity. Because of them, I am able to live my life with a compelling drive and clarity that I hope honors them. And as I navigate the paths of my own journey, they left me with an assurance, a sort of Blessed Assurance that continues to author my life.

This is my love story to *Mama 'n Nem*.

Mama 'n 'Nem

HANDPRINTS ON MY LIFE

All the rivers run into the sea,
yet the sea is not full;
unto the place from whence the rivers come,
thither they return again.

ECCLESIASTES 1:7

CHAPTER ONE

Mama

CIRCLE OF LIFE

She openeth her mouth with wisdom;
and in her tongue is the law of kindness.
She looketh well to the ways of her household,
and eateth not the bread of idleness.
The heart of her husband doth safely trust in her.
Her children arise up and call her blessed.

PROVERBS 31: 26, 27, 11, 28

The trees that lined the cemetery were magnificent. Their trunks were fierce and wide. Their branches were like emaciated fingers stretching high into the heavens. The day seemed angry as the motorcade slowly made its way around the winding path to Mama's grave site. It was wickedly cold. And the overcast sky gave no relief from its constant drizzle. The fine mist felt like tiny needle pricks on my face as the Chicago wind bore down.

When we reached the open grave, a host of family and friends gathered under the frail canopy. It was all so surreal, like it wasn't really Mama we were laying to rest. The preacher began his final ritual. And for several moments, it's as if time stood still for me, like everything just stopped. There was no talking, no wind, no weeping, no rain. There was a hush, a quiet, a stillness. And hundreds of the most vivid memories flashed through my mind. It was only a precious few moments, but a personal gift to me direct from the hand of God. The wind blew viciously, leaving a dusting of autumn leaves on the grave tops. I felt something warm wash over me, and then . . . time began again. The spoken ritual ended, and handfuls of dirt were thrown as we said our last goodbyes.

When I remember the day, the details are vivid and clear like it was just yesterday. But every image is played out in black and white, except for the dozens of red roses that were thrown as Mama's casket was lowered into the ground.

Emma Jean was the baby of the Whitlock family and adored by all, especially her father Samuel, who proclaimed early on that she would be called simply "Em." Throughout childhood, she was feared by all the boys in the neighborhood because she stood up to them and never lost a fight. Aunt Sky said the boys picked on her because she was too pretty. She was thin and golden-brown, with a wide smile. And she had big brown eyes shaped like almonds. Her thick black hair was always in a single braid hanging down her back. Whenever Clemmuel Lacy got the chance, he would yank her braid and take off running. The last time he did that deed, he turned to run and tripped over his own shoelace. She pummeled him good that day. After that, despite teasing from the other boys, they became the best of friends. Twelve years would go by before Clemmuel Lacy asked for her hand in marriage.

Upon finishing her studies at Arkansas AM&N College, and receiving a degree in early childhood education, she and her mother began planning for a June wedding. The grounds of the modest Whitlock farm were transformed to host the wedding and reception. The front of the house was given a fresh coat of white paint. The banisters on the front porch were draped on either side with yards of billowing white tulle, donated by the local haberdashery. The trees leading up to the house were wrapped with white ribbon. The chicken coop was moved to the back of the house, and Big Papa's rusty trucks were rolled out of sight behind the old barn.

A bridal shower was given the day before the wedding, attended only by close friends and family. Each woman came bearing a very personal gift for the bride: a camisole, a slip, an embroidered handkerchief. After all the gifts were opened, Big Mama sent for the hope chest. It was the same chest she had used to gather things for the marriages of all her girls. Big Papa hand made it out of rich oak. On it, he carved symbols representing family members—some passed on, some living. And whenever a new baby was born, he would carve a new symbol on the old chest, honoring the circle of life. Big Papa set the chest in the center of the room, kissed his youngest daughter, and left the women to their ceremony.

With all her sisters married, Mama was the last of the Whitlock girls to receive the hope chest. It was a time of expectation, of change and new life. Mama would receive her rite of passage, as each of her sisters had. The candles were lit, the lights were dimmed, and each woman held the hand of another woman, creating a circle around the room. As Big Mama began the ritual, there was a break in her voice and tears welled up in her eyes as she contemplated her baby girl leaving the homestead and moving to Chicago, as the other girls had done. This would be the last time she would render this rite of passage, this sacred gift.

Her daughters flocked to her side: Mama, Tee, Sky, Sadie, and Mae. And as they all embraced and wiped away tears, the sisters made an inner circle around their mother, surrounding her with love and strength. And she began the ritual again: "A woman is precious in the sight of God. She is fearfully and wonderfully made. Her husband is the giver, and she is the receiver. Marriage is but a dance between two people, each moving to the rhythm of the other. . . ."

At the end of the ceremony, the celebrated chest was opened. It was filled with practical things needed by every new bride: linens and towels, the Holy Bible. But Big Mama had also stashed away in this ornate box some of the loveliest things for her baby girl. There were dozens of embroidered tea towels, French lace handkerchiefs, three pairs of silk stockings, a white lace and linen nightgown Big

Mama had made special for the wedding night. A quilt she had been working on for months was at the very bottom of the chest. It was the *piece d'resistance*. Big Mama made a unique quilt for each of her girls that was presented to her on the eve of her wedding. The women oohed and ahhed as this exquisite quilt in the palest of blues was stretched out for all to see. And as always, the evening ended with prayer and words of wisdom to the bride from the elders.

Big Mama, her sisters, and the women in the community prepared an overabundance of food for the hundred-odd guests in attendance. Mama was radiant in a white satin and tulle gown. Her sisters were her bridesmaids, and Daddy's brothers were his groomsmen. The celebration lasted well into the night. There was toasting and line dancing, and the children enjoyed catching fireflies and hours of hide and seek. Finally, the couple said their goodbyes and left all things familiar to embark upon their new life together. And as the car pulled away, Big Papa stood in the doorway to see the newlyweds off. He stayed in that spot long after their car was out of sight. Only after the tears stopped coming was he able to go inside.

CHAPTER TWO

Daddy

LIFE LESSONS

Children's children are the crown of old men;
and the glory of children are their fathers.

PROVERBS 17: 6

I grew up the fourth of five children, and in all my childhood years my father never once said, "I love you." But, somehow, I always knew I was loved.

Clemmuel Randolph Lacy was born the sixth of eleven children to Oscar and Genevieve Lacy, and at an early age he became the patriarch of the family. Daddy was the eldest son still at home when his father died. His older brothers were off giving service to the United States Army. So at the age of thirteen he dropped out of school and took a job on the railroad to support his mother and younger siblings.

As far back as I can remember, Daddy was always a maintenance man, a painter, a garbage man, a Mister Fix-it, or what some would call a jack-of-all-trades. We were born and raised in Chicago—all over Chicago. Daddy was usually the super of a residential building. We could stay in one of the apartments rent-free, as long as his work was up to par and management didn't change.

My first memory of life with Daddy is when I was about three years old. We lived in a third floor apartment over a store on West

Madison Street in Chicago. It was a spacious, three-bedroom apartment with worn hardwood floors and leaky radiators. The flowered wallpaper was dingy and faded. But it was warm and cozy, filled with Big Mama's old furniture. There were four of us kids at the time, each one of us a year apart. There was me (Greta), Shane, Clem Jr., and my sister Hazel.

We weren't allowed to go outside because there was no front or back yard to play in, only the busy Madison Street thoroughfare. So the apartment was our playground. We loved playing together, but we fought like cats and dogs. We teamed up against each other, boys against the girls, but like typical siblings we stuck up for one another. We'd beat each other down, but nobody else could.

Most days Daddy would bring us penny candy or inexpensive treats when he'd come home from work. And we'd sit in a circle on the floor and trade Mary Janes for Wine Candies or Tootsie Rolls for Bazooka bubble gum. Sometimes he'd bring us balloons to play with. Some were so big, we'd blow them up and we'd bounce around the apartment all day. Mama said we were always under foot.

As a child, I was fascinated with fire, especially fire that came out of the eyes on the stove. Its base was a beautiful blue, but the tips burned yellow, orange, and red. The colors fusing together mesmerized me. When Mama cooked, I would stand and stare at the fire, transfixed by the tiny inferno. Despite her warnings about the searing heat of the fire, on several occasions she caught me reaching out, trying to touch it. My respect for fire came at about age four. The last time I attempted to touch the blue flames, Mama made it her business to tell Daddy.

When he came home from work, he seemed unusually quiet. But after dinner, Daddy was talkative and playful. He bounced me around on his knee, swept me up in his arms, and took me into the kitchen. He turned on an eye very low on the stove and held my small hand over the flame.

"Is that hot? Huh? You see how hot that is? If that fire get on you, it'll burn you to death, and we'll have to bury you and put you in the ground. And we'll still have to pour water over that dirt to cool you off!"

By this time I was kicking and screaming, "Please, Daddy, I ain't gone do it no more. I ain't gone do it no more!"

But my snot-filled cries for mercy were for naught. I was desperately trying to pull my hand away from the flame, but there was no budging his massive hand. It was only a few seconds, but it seemed like hours. When he released his grip, I coiled into him, terrified by the experience. Daddy was a strict and firm teacher, but he knew it would be a lesson well learned. After giving me over to Mama, who was in tears, he repeated the act with the rest of my siblings, so he'd never have to teach that lesson again.

It was a lazy, sun-drenched, summer afternoon and, as always, we couldn't go outside. We were going stir crazy. Mama was talking on the phone to Aunt Mae while cooking dinner. We found some balloons in a drawer and someone said, "Hey, let's make water balloons and drop 'em out the front window."

I wasn't allowed to participate, because I couldn't tie a knot in the balloons, and I was too young to play near the open window. But I squealed with joy as I watched the balloons being filled and tied, hauled over to the window, and strategically dropped. The boys would spot an unsuspecting target, drop the watery bomb, and quickly duck inside. Once we heard the sound of the balloon breaking, a surprised yelp, scream, or angry expletive immediately followed. We laughed so hard our bellies ached. We'd wait until the coast was clear and gleefully do it again. That was absolutely the most fun we'd ever had in that third floor apartment until Daddy walked in.

"What y'all doin'? Didn't I tell you not to play in that window? Huh? Y'all droppin' them balloons out that window?"

We were stunned into silence. We couldn't lie, because Shane was holding a fat water balloon with both hands, and three others were poised in a bowl on the floor. How did he always know? It's like he had radar that signaled him whenever we were having too much fun, or what he would call misbehaving. He took us by our feet and, one by one, hung us out that third floor window, fussing throughout.

"You see how high this is? This window ain't nothin' to be playin' in. You fool around and fall, ain't nothing the doctors can do."

We screamed for our lives, and passersby stopped in horror to watch. Madison Street was a terrifying view from upside down. Mama tucked us all in that night with her soothing voice and tears in her eyes and reassured us that Daddy never would have dropped us. She said that he wasn't being mean, but loved us very much and just wanted to teach us a lesson. Lesson learned.

We were brought up in what some folks call the Sanctified Church. We were austerely religious "Holy Rollers." The ordinary things our peers did were forbidden to us. We couldn't go to the movies or parties or have friends sleep over. Daddy said secular songs were the devil's music, and it would not be tolerated in his house.

One time Mama and Daddy went to take care of some business and left Hazel in charge. He said they'd be back in a couple of hours. When the coast was clear, Shane put on a James Brown 45 he had found in the alley. If this was the devil's music, it sure felt good to our souls. How liberating! We played "Hot Pants" over and over again until we had worked ourselves up into a silly frenzy. We clapped and bucked and stomped and gyrated and popped our fingers. And when James Brown would scream, we'd scream too. We were in mid-scream and full buck when the front door opened. Everything after that seemed to go in slow motion: Daddy crossing from the front door to the record player, the breaking of the record, the cracking of the razor strap across our butts. It didn't matter that Shane was the one who brought the record home. If one was guilty, everybody was guilty. Once Clem Jr. brought home a deck of cards to play Solitaire or Go Fish, but they were immediately thrown out because cards were associated with gambling. My sister and I were forbidden to wear pants, or nail polish of any kind. And sandals were strictly taboo. Daddy said toeless and heelless shoes drew a man's attention to a woman's feet and legs.

Daddy loved to cook. And he was good at it. So, when Mr. Frasier, a long-time friend of the family, fell into bad health and needed to sell his restaurant, Daddy seized the opportunity. He negotiated with him and got it for a good price. It was on the corner of 73rd and Halsted. He branded it Randolph's Restaurant & Sundries.

I remember the first time I saw the sign hand painted on the window, I asked, "Daddy, who is Randolph, and what are sundries?"

He chuckled indulgently and said, "Randolph, well, you're lookin' at him. I've never had an opportunity to use my middle name. My mother loved that name. So, I thought this was a good way to kind of honor her. And sundries are all the little miscellaneous things we sell up front, like gum, aspirin, cigarettes, and so on."

The restaurant was long and narrow. Just inside its doors, at the right, was a little six-by-six area of shelves filled with odds and ends. Beyond that was a long counter with eight chrome stools that shined—but more importantly, they swiveled. On the other side were eight square tables for dining in. Randolph's Restaurant & Sundries was open six days a week, Monday through Saturday— Daddy had to preach on Sundays—from 7:00 a.m. till 6:00 p.m. Sometimes Mama would take us after closing, so as not to interfere with the paying customers. We always sat at the counter. We'd take turns spinning each other on the stools to see who could get the dizziest. Daddy would make us hamburgers, French fries, and grilled cheese sandwiches. Then we'd watch him break down the grill and scrub it with steel wool 'til it gleamed like new money.

Two years would go by, and the little corner restaurant was holding its own. Daddy hired a dishwasher and a waitress to help him with the day-to-day operations. The busiest time was breakfast. And Daddy was a master at preparing perfect crispy bacon, savory sausages and fried ham, fluffy grits, hash browns, and eggs any style.

It was a good volume day. Daddy said lots of customers were dining in, but even more were calling in orders for takeout. The day was winding down. The dishwasher was done for the day, and the waitress was cashing out the last two dine-in customers. After counting her tips, she clocked out and said good night. As Daddy was locking the door behind her, a young woman approached the threshold. "Sir, can you help me? I'm hungry."

He carefully inspected her from head to toe. She looked weary and disheveled, and, among other things, it seemed as if she was in dire need of a meal. He unlocked the door and motioned her over to the counter. He gave her a piece of corn bread, which she greedily consumed. He warmed up some left-over pork chops with string beans and macaroni and cheese, and set the piping hot food in front of her. He smiled humbly, as he watched her voraciously devour the provisions. He gave her a tall glass of iced tea to wash it all down and asked her if she would like a care package to go. She nodded eagerly, wiping her mouth with her sleeve.

Daddy went to work preparing some cold cut sandwiches. He made sure she had a few bags of potato chips, and some sodas. Just as he was placing some napkins in the bag, he felt the cold, hard steel on the back of his neck. "Thank you. I'll take that," she said. A chill zigzagged up his spine, as he turned to face the barrel of the gun. She took the bag and waved him towards the cash register and ordered him to empty it. As he did, she unlocked the door, and a tall, gaunt man skulked in. The accomplice took over the well-thought-out robbery and began filling his duffle bag with the money from the register. Daddy watched helplessly as the two thieves stole a whole day's worth of work that amounted to hundreds of dollars. The criminals fled on foot, carrying our livelihood and the care package of food Daddy had prepared.

When the police arrived, the thieves were long gone, but the damage left in their wake was ever-present. Never again did Daddy enjoy his time at Randolph's. Every customer was a potential threat until their bill was paid and they had left the premises. Mama urged him to sell the restaurant. She said it wasn't wise or healthy to live with that kind of fear every day. About eight months to the day after that robbery, Daddy gave up the restaurant business, just walked away from it and once again took a job as a super of a thirty-unit apartment complex.

One of Daddy's cardinal rules was: No sleepovers. Period. And we didn't sleep at other people's houses either. My girlfriend Veronica had come over after Vacation Bible School. I finished my chores early, and Mama let us eat dinner in my room. We giggled and gossiped and talked about boys till well past 9:00 p.m. Since it was too late for Veronica to catch the bus, I asked Daddy if he would take her home. "How did she get here?" he grumbled. Daddy was suspect of everybody until you proved to him otherwise. On the way to Veronica's house we sat in the back and giggled and whispered and giggled some more, mostly about boys.

Finally, Veronica blurted out, "Mr. Lacy, can I spend the night sometime?"

And without taking a breath, Daddy replied, "No." His response wasn't mean, but direct and matter-of-fact.

"Why?" She asked.

"Because if I let you spend the night at our house, eventually you're gonna want Greta to spend the night at yours. So to keep the devil at bay, its best that she lay her head on her own pillow at night. Cause if you let the devil ride, after while he's gone wanna drive."

Veronica and I looked at each other, snickered and shrugged our shoulders. We hadn't a clue what he was talking about.

That was the summer Big Papa died. And we all made the pilgrimage down to Wilmar, Arkansas, for the home going. It had all the makings of a summer vacation or a big, fat family reunion. Daddy stacked shoe boxes full of sandwiches and fried chicken in the back of the station wagon. There was a cooler packed to the brim with fruit, juice, and sodas. We loved that station wagon because it had an extra seat in the rear that faced the back of the car. Oh, the fun we had making faces at the drivers and passengers in the car that followed! The best part of the trip was enjoying a respite at the rest stops. The caravan of cars would unload the food at the picnic tables provided and have a giant-sized pot luck. It was a long trip, with miles and miles of trees, corn fields, and things I had only seen on TV, like herds of horses and cattle.

Finally we pulled off the highway onto a long, winding, dirt road. We came to a clearing. When the cloud of dust from the caravan cleared, there stood a modest white house with two sprawling maple trees on either side framing it perfectly. The simplicity and symmetry of it was breathtaking. Miss Willa Dee was on the porch waving welcome to us. She was Big Papa's wife of fifteen years. He married her two years after Big Mama died. She beckoned us to pull around back between a small trailer house and the old chicken coop. Most of the family stayed in the house, but we stayed in the trailer. It was cramped and creaky, but neat and clean. Not long after we arrived, Hazel and I found great pleasure in chasing the chickens around the yard until Miss Willa Dee scolded us and herded the chickens back in the coop and slammed the gate. It had been such an eventful day, sleep didn't come easy that night. Through the open windows of the trailer we could hear hoots and caws and purrs from creatures that weren't indigenous to the city.

The morning ushered in a brand new day and with it a somberness. The men wore black suits. The women adorned themselves in black dresses and matching hats with veils that hid bloodshot eyes and mournful tears. The little chapel where Big Papa lay was packed with family and friends. At eighty-two, he had lived a good life, the reverend said. He had been a devoted father, a good friend, and a model citizen in the community, and he would be sorely missed. After the choir sang and a final prayer was given, we began our procession to the cemetery. It was a small plot of land behind the tiny chapel that held the remains of the notable Blacks in Wilmar. Big Mama had been laid to rest there seventeen years before. But Miss Willa Dee had taken measures to ensure that Big Papa's grave was nowhere near his first wife's. She buried him on a lowly hill by himself. She said she wanted his final resting place to have prominence, but it was clear what her motive was.

Miss Willa Dee was an odd specimen. She wasn't fair to look upon, but not totally unattractive. She wasn't fat, but she was big-boned. She wore her hair in a tight French roll, so her features looked severe. Mama said she was a hoo doo, woman—someone who practiced voodoo or black magic. It was rumored that she killed her first husband. One day, after months of quarrelling, they say she left him in their bedroom, walked out the front door, and seconds later the house went up in flames. There was a creepiness about her. She had an icy demeanor, and it seemed as if her tiny eyes bore right through you. I watched her intently. Whenever we sat down for a meal and a blessing was said, she excused herself from the room. Shane and I were convinced she was a witch. She seemed to be repelled by any mention of God.

The next morning we packed up the cars in preparation for our journey north. Miss Willa Dee stood on the porch and, just as she had waved us welcome, she now stood and bid us farewell. Mama said it looked like she was waving us good riddance.

CHAPTER THREE

Woman's Intuition
& NEW BEGINNINGS

Mama finally landed a job as an elementary school teacher at Susan B. Anthony on Chicago's west side. In the mid 1960s, the school had just become integrated. But with the huge migration of the Negro from the South to the North, Susan B. Anthony became an all-Black school in a matter of a few years.

When I was about age seven, sometimes Mama would take me to school with her. That was always such a treat. She'd let me pick out a dress the night before, and she'd starch and iron it and lay it out with crisp white socks. We'd get up extra early the next morning to prepare for the day. After a quick bath and breakfast, Mama would let me dress myself, and then she would run a warm comb through my hair just to straighten it a bit. I loved going to Susan B. Anthony. I felt like a celebrity. All the teachers knew me by name and would give me a quarter or fifty cents just because. With the money, I would always buy those amazing butter cookies only Lunchroom Ladies know how to make.

Mama was probably one of the wisest women I've ever known—and funnnnny! We could always count on Mama to drop her pearls of wisdom when she felt the situation warranted it. She'd rattle off things like: "Sweep around your own front door before you try to sweep around mine." "While you busy pointing your finger at somebody else, there are always three fingers pointing right back at you." "If you'll lie, you'll steal." "It's a poor wind that don't change sometime." "It's just nice to be nice." "Every tub has to sit on it's own bottom." And in an effort to get us to bathe regularly she'd say: "Cleanliness is next to Godliness. And God ain't gone have nobody stinkin' in heaven."

Mama was a woman of great faith. She radiated peace and tranquility. I always sensed angels hovering about her, imbuing her with serenity and lacing her words with grace. But she also relied on her instincts and intuition to give her insight to discern people and their intentions.

Now, Priscilla Dent was a saleswoman for the Amway Company. (She sold their products door to door.) She had spoken to Daddy about becoming an Amway distributor and had set up a meeting to discuss it further. Mama was ambivalent because Daddy had attempted previous similar ventures that had ended disastrously. When Priscilla Dent arrived at the apartment, she was dressed in a grey business suit that fit her like a glove. A string of pearls hung gracefully around her neck, and the tight pencil skirt stopped just above her knees. She wore her hair natural. It was very short, cut and tapered like a man's. But she was all womanly and sensuous. And she held us all captive for an hour as she pitched the Amway line, crossing and uncrossing her legs. When she finished her presentation, I wanted to sell Amway products. Mama was very reluctant, but Daddy was sold. Over the next several months, the apartment became overrun with boxes upon boxes of Amway products. We were receiving merchandise faster than Daddy could sell it.

Finally, Mama had enough. She told him emphatically that he was spending too much time away from home at these Amway meetings and much too much time with Priscilla Dent. "I didn't like her from day one. That hussy flounced her ball-headed self in here with her tight suit on, lookin' like a weasel about the face. I didn't trust her then, and I don't trust her now. Clem, you can deny it all you want, but that woman is after you! We haven't seen any of the bonuses she promised. But she keeps you collecting inventory and following up behind her to these meetings. I want all traces of Ms. Priscilla out of my house and my life, with her mannish self. What woman wears her hair that short? She reminds me of one o' them ole bulldaggers."

Daddy attempted to defend Priscilla Dent. "Now, Em, Priscilla ain't no bulldagger, she is my boss. And I have to attend these meetings to keep abreast of changes and new information."

Daddy was aware that Mama emphasized "Ms." when she last referred to Priscilla. "And Priscilla ain't married 'cause she's a business woman. She says she enjoys her independence 'cause she's free to do whatever she . . ." The look on Mama's face undoubtedly spoke volumes. She had a way of communicating loudly and clearly without ever saying a word. Priscilla Dent's name was dropped and never mentioned again. That tie had been unequivocally severed. The Amway products were discounted and sold at the annual church bazaar, and Mama included them as stocking stuffers that Christmas.

From kindergarten to sixth grade, Bass Elementary School was home to me. In an effort to make class sizes smaller, several mobile units were built in a corner of the parking lot, and students were divided between regular classrooms and the new glorified trailers. I was one of the students selected to go to Mrs. Jackson's sixth grade class, trailer #3. Everything smelled so new: the carpet, the desks, even the #2 pencils she passed out welcoming us on our first day. Mrs. Jackson was tall for a woman, about six feet. She had red hair, a toothy grin, and she always looked over her glasses when she talked.

The mobile units were small. The desks had to be butted up against each other, so your elbows literally touched the person next to you. To my left was Steven Brown, a curly-haired boy with nice eyes and a friendly demeanor. To my right was Karen Adams. I remembered seeing her around the school yard. We became fast friends. She was an only child, her mother was also a school teacher, and I wanted to be her because she wore a different outfit to school every day.

Like always, the bell rang at 3:15. I said goodbye to my new friends Karen and Steven, and began my walk home. Just as I got to the last mobile unit, I was approached by two classmates who sat directly across from me. The shorter one was Connie Williamson, whose reputation for being a bully was the talk of the school. She was menacing. She had a short afro and a wide nose. When she talked, her voice was deep and husky. And I couldn't stop looking at her mouth because her lips seemed to take up her entire face. Her tall side-kick was Lorena Salter. She was easily six feet tall, and the sheer mass of her was intimidating to say the least. Connie did all the talking. She began, "Somebody told me you was trying to steal my boyfriend. And I don't take lightly to nobody trying to steal my boyfriend."

I had no idea what she was talking about, so I innocently asked her, "Who is your boyfriend?"

"Steven," she said.

I was dumbfounded. I had just met him that day. The only thing we had done was exchange pleasantries. Lorena never said a word, just nodded occasionally in agreement. I was so petrified my knees began to knock against each other. I remember babbling on about how I didn't like Steven, and that he'd only let me use one of his crayons because I didn't have yellow. They finally ended their interrogation and left. When I got to the edge of the parking lot, I ran all the way home. The next day it happened again, and the day after that, and the day after that. Four weeks went by, and the bullies terrorized me almost daily, leaving a cloud of palpable fear in their wake.

It was a Friday, and the clock inevitably struck 3:15. The way the classroom was set up, I was always one of the first students to leave. That day, intuitively I knew I had to get a good head start. Once outside, I broke out running. I whizzed by the first mobile unit, the second, and the third, but somehow they headed me off at the fourth. Lorena knocked my books out of my hands, and Connie shoved me up against the trailer. And the interrogation began. "I heard you was talkin' about my Mama!" And a barrage of "No, I wasn't," "Yes, you was," "No, I wasn't," "Yes, you was" ensued. And with every accusation, Connie knocked the back of my head against the trailer. After the thirteenth blow, I began to see stars. On the fourteenth, a still small voice said loudly, "Duck!" When she came in for the fifteenth blow, I dropped. And before they knew it, I was gone. I thought, "If I can just get to the corner store, I'll be safe." But just as I turned the corner out of the school yard, I slipped on the gravel and fell. The two bullies were just about to pummel me when they were stopped by a woman carrying a baby. She marched us all off to the principal's office.

Connie and Lorena's parents couldn't be reached, but they were promptly sent home, suspended for a month. When Mama came to pick me up, my right knee was bloody from the fall, and my pants were wet. Somewhere during the traumatic episode I had apparently peed on myself. I sat in the hall while Mama talked to the principal in private.

Once home, she started dinner and then concentrated on my wounds, physical and emotional. She cleaned and sterilized the area with warm water and Mercurochrome, then made a poultice and wrapped my knee in gauze. As she lovingly tended to my injury, she quietly asked why I had never said anything about the bullying. Connie's older brother was a member of the Black Stone Rangers. She said if I told, her brother and his gang would make life a living hell for my entire family. Mama scoffed at the notion and said I mustn't let a little sixth grade girl torment me in such a way. She said, "Bullies are usually people with low self esteem, and they torture others because, in some twisted way, it makes them feel better about themselves." The very next morning Mama transferred me from Bass Elementary to Garrett A. Morgan Middle School.

The smell of newly laid carpet permeated the air as Mama and I strolled through the doors of Garrett A. Morgan. I was relieved to be leaving my bullies behind and thrilled to see what this new learning environment would bring. The structure was only four months old, and everything was sparkly and bright. The lunchroom was a huge open space. It seemed ascetically sterile like a hospital, because everything was white and stainless steel. Even the lunchroom ladies in their white uniforms reminded me of nurses as they went about their day. The gymnasium still smelled of fresh paint and shellac. From one end of the gym to the other the floor was like a colossal mirror. I remember chuckling to myself when I saw my reflection as we walked through on our tour. The classrooms were open and airy with lots of sunlight streaming through the oversized windows.

I settled into Room 201 with a teacher I was sure I didn't like. Ms. Ann Brown was a character to say the least. On the first day I called her Mrs. Brown, and she hastily corrected me. "My name is Ms. Brown. I'm not married; never have been. I'm a single mother and proud of it." She was tall and thin, with manly hands and big feet. She had short cropped hair and teeth that were a little too big for her mouth. The length of her sleeves and pants were always a couple of inches too short, and her makeup was so severe it was rumored that she used to be Anthony Brown. She was loud and rude and matter-of-fact. We had reflection time every day where we discussed everything from religion to masturbation, and I was usually appalled and intellectually stimulated at the same time.

Ms. Brown immediately took to me because of something I had never been acknowledged for before—my penmanship. She praised me for the shape and slant of the letters, and overall neatness and precision. And I loved her for that. I quickly became the "teacher's pet." She called on me to do any and all writing on the blackboard. And when she changed out her bulletin boards, I was the chosen one. She sent me on special errands to the principal's office and the teacher's lounge, and many times I sat with her at her desk and helped her grade papers. The students looked up to me, and that gave me a confidence you can't measure. Beyond my penmanship, Ms. Brown saw something in me that she wanted to cultivate, and for that I will be forever grateful.

The playground was full of life: girls jumping double-dutch, boys playing basketball. The monkey bars were full of bodies and hands. There was squealing on swings high in the air, and the noisy seesaw rocked back and forth. Recess was the best time of the school day. It was my turn to jump rope when she walked onto the playground. I fell in love with her before I'd even met her. She stood about five feet four inches tall. She had honey-colored skin and the prettiest smile I'd ever seen in my life. She wore a leopard-print coat, with black patent leather boots. Her hair was in two tight pony tails, and attached to them were curly afro puffs. I remember thinking to myself, "Who lets their seventh grader wear makeup and fake hair?" She was wearing blue eye shadow, black eye liner, and lip gloss. I so wanted to be her.

An inquisitive group gathered around the new girl. Her name was Sylvia Parson. What a grown up name for a little girl! But it fit her perfectly, because she was mature and polite and oh so lady-like. I invited her to sit with me during lunch period and discovered her father was also pastor of a small church. How was I to know that encounter would spark a friendship that would last a lifetime? After my dad met Reverend Parson, Sylvia and I became joined at the hip. We did everything together: movies, shopping, eating, singing, church-visiting, dating. Yes, we went on dates together— well, they were her dates; I was always the tag-a-long. Her parents wouldn't have had it any other way. Boys were just drawn to her, like bees to honey. She possessed something elusive I didn't have, but I loved being in her company, hoping some of it would rub off on me.

On my twelfth birthday Daddy was installed as pastor of Morning Star Church of God in Christ. It was a small storefront church on the south side of Chicago that had recently lost its pastor to cancer. The tiny house of worship was packed to capacity, creating a vibrant portrait of the perfect church tableau: choir robes, ushers, a mourner's bench, and ladies in church hats fanning themselves copiously.

Reverend Parson brought his entire family to celebrate with us. Sylvia and I sat together on the left side of the church near the organ. Just before the keynote speaker brought his message, he called on his wife for words of exhortation. She began, "Giving honor to God, who is the head of my life, to my own pastor, to all of the pastors, missionaries, and the ecclesia of the most high: We are happy to be here to honor Reverend Lacy as he puts on the whole armor of God and as he shods his feet with the preparation of the gospel of peace. I am overjoyed to see these benches filled up!"

At that moment, Sylvia nudged me, and, before we could quench it, one of our irrepressible laugh affairs began. She continued, "Praise God! As I look around this church, every bench in here is filled!" By that time we were shaking uncontrollably. In an effort to save face, I had fallen over on my pew, and Sylvia followed, shuddering on my left side. It was hilarious to us because she kept referring to the pews as benches, which sounded like "bitches." We finally collected ourselves. Just as we sat up straight in our pew she said, "It is my prayer that from now on, every bench in here is overflowing!" Sylvia fell to the opposite side, and I was now quaking beside her. Good times.

Daddy had worked faithfully for several years as an elder at its sister church, Christ Temple Church in Evanston, Illinois. He had always wanted his own church. He said good preaching was food for the soul. Pastoring his own church was a dream come true. But that dream quickly faded. Morning Star was a small, family church. Its deceased former pastor was also its founder, who had left behind a controlling wife, her seven sisters, and their hosts of children and grandchildren. From the beginning, it was us against them, Davids against Goliaths, literally. The Church Sisters—Jilly, Corinth, Alice, Bertha, Dorthea, Alberta, Ethel, and Gladys—were enormous, embittered women who always had a chip on their shoulder or an ax to grind. Daddy was just a figure-head, appointed only because the denomination did not allow women to pastor its churches. But it had its advantages. The title of pastor was prestigious. Daddy represented the church at local and national meetings. And once a year he'd be honored with a Pastor's Anniversary Celebration where the entire offertory would go to him.

But most of the time, we were in servitude. Whenever the church doors opened we had to be there, even if nobody else showed up. And sometimes nobody else did. We were little ushers and deacons, choir members, money counters, and devotion leaders. We also cleaned the bathrooms, mopped the floors, cut the grass, chopped down weeds, and helped with countless chicken dinner fundraisers. Daddy was pastor, but also the resident plumber, painter, carpenter, and electrician. There was no salary, only an offering collected for him once a month. It was never enough. So he always juggled his day job with the highly stressful job of pastoring a small storefront church.

Between the Church Sisters, they had about fifty children. The one I remember most is Jilly's teenage daughter Roberta. She was gargantuan in size. She easily weighed 300 pounds, wore a perpetual scowl on her face, and she had the worst breath I'd ever smelled, like she was rotting from the inside out. The sheer mass of her made all the other kids clear a way to let her pass when she entered a room. One day, during Vacation Bible School, Roberta walked into the lunch area on a mission, like a dinosaur looking to seek out and devour its prey. As she purposefully scanned the room, her eyes caught mine, and before I could look away she began walking towards me. I remember her massive shadow overtaking me even before she did. As this female giant stood in front of me, I slowly lifted my head to meet her gaze. "Gimme a bite of that pickle," she demanded. I couldn't say no. She was scary and much bigger than me. I hadn't even taken a bite myself. But I handed over my sour pickle with a new peppermint stick in the middle. She took a hefty bite, and, just like that, half the pickle and the peppermint stick were gone. She shoved the remaining half in my hand, and she and her massive shadow skulked away. I was mad, but even more horrified when I lifted my pickle to inspect it further, and smelled the residue of her breath lingering on its pitiful remains. I left the lunchroom line and threw the pickle away. I wasn't hungry anymore.

There were countless church events to attend. There were teas and luncheons, banquets and anniversaries, musicals and conventions, cotillions and Easter programs, Christmas pageants, weddings and funerals. The Church Sisters' family was so large, there was always somebody dying, and Daddy was always called on to give the eulogy at the home going service.

And the Church Sisters were screamers. At every funeral, without fail, one would start wailing, followed by the others, with blood curdling screams, laying over the coffin, pleading with the deceased not to go, and many times passing out cold. There was always a rush of ushers and morticians to lovingly remove hysterical family members and revive the fainted. I hated it. I would sit stunned and terrified. But Daddy said death was a part of life, and we should be there to pay last respects to our church member's dearly departed loved one. When we got home, after it was all said and done, the burial and repast, Mama would tuck me in to bed and leave the light on because I could see the coffin too clearly in the dark. Sometimes I would be so scared, Daddy would let me slip into Mama's side of the bed and I'd finally drop off to sleep. And I never understood the whole repast thing—how people could eat, drink, and be merry after burying someone they loved.

Although the Church Sisters were controlling, mean, and often down right scary, when they cooked I'm certain the heavens opened up so the angels could smell the aroma. Soul Food never tasted so good: fried chicken, candied yams, macaroni and cheese, collard greens, corn bread, chicken tetrazini, black-eyed peas, string beans and white potatoes, peach cobbler, pound cake, sweet potato pie. And Jilly's yeast rolls were so light and sweet and buttery, they literally melted in your mouth. During the three years at Morning Star, the Church Sisters never showed us outward signs of love. But somehow we tasted it in every dish they prepared. Mama said she suspected that was the only way they knew how to show it.

CHAPTER FOUR

Aunt Tee

SEQUINS & BEADS

She stretcheth out her hand to the poor;
yea, she reacheth forth her hands to the needy.
Give her the fruit of her hands;
and let her own works praise her in the gates.

PROVERBS 31: 20, 3122

Aunt Tee was my favorite aunt. Born Nellie Zunobia Whitlock, she hated her first and middle names and preferred to be called Tee. She was a beautician by trade and did hair out of her kitchen. Mama would always take me with her to Aunt Tee's to get her hair done. On Saturdays, Daddy would drop us off, and Tobby and I got to play together for hours. Mama, her sisters, and scores of women in the community would converge in Aunt Tee's kitchen to get their hair done and talk grown-folks business. There'd be lots of neighborhood and family gossip swirling about. They'd shoo us out of the room if they sensed we were listening.

Tobby was a year older than me, but we were a match made in heaven. He'd play the piano, and I'd sing. We'd play hide and seek or jump on the indoor trampoline. Aunt Tee was extremely overprotective of Tobby. He was never allowed to go outside to play. All activities were kept indoors. So the trampoline was in the basement.

And because the ceiling was so low, we never experienced the sheer pleasure of jumping high.

Aunt Tee was round and fair skinned, with slanted eyes that smiled even when she wasn't. She had a gorgeous head of hair, but she always wore a wig. The mane of the wig likened her own tresses—long, curly, and jet-black. Mama would say, "Tee's always doin' somebody else's head, that's why she never has time to fix her own." Aunt Tee was the most giving person I've ever known. She was always cooking and sending food to the sick and shut in. She'd prepare and sell dinners out of her home to help people with their rent and utilities. Sometimes she'd walk up to you and discreetly press a hundred dollar bill into your hand and say, "Take it. The Lord told me to bless you."

Aunt Tee was plump and only about five feet tall, but she had a great sense of style. She had expensive furs and beautiful jewelry. She also had an extensive collection of clothes with shoes, pocketbooks, and hats to match. I loved playing dress-up in Aunt Tee's closet. It was a menagerie of wonderful things that had a certain feel and smell to them. The shelves were lined with exquisite pointed-toed pumps made of sequins and beads and fine leathers, all size 6-1/2. Mama said Aunt Tee really wore a size 7, but she liked her shoes a half size smaller. She said it made her light on her feet and made her tip like a princess when she walked.

When Aunt Tee stepped out to church or any function, she was dressed impeccably. When she entered a banquet hall, people would stop eating. If she tipped in late to church, the preacher would stop preaching and acknowledge her presence. Aunt Tee could make an entrance effortlessly. Her clothes weren't flashy or gaudy, but screamed quiet elegance. And beyond her stylish exterior, she embodied something that was extraordinary and intangible that every woman who encountered her wanted to possess. She's the only woman I've ever known who seemed to alter the air as she moved through it. She was always sweet and soft spoken. There was nothing loud about Aunt Tee except her praise for the Lord.

Sometimes during church service Aunt Tee would be overcome with the Spirit, and she'd dance ever so lightly in her tiny little pumps up and down the aisles, her black curls bouncing gingerly around her shoulders, shouting, "Praise Jesus, Wonderful Savior."

Much of who Aunt Tee was could be seen just stepping into her living room. Each piece of furniture was French Provincial, exquisite and massive in scale. The sofa and chairs were upholstered in rich cream damask, with bits of gold running through. They were carefully covered in clear plastic for their preservation. Two giant stone lamps flanked either side of the sofa, their shades just inches from the ceiling. Facing the sofa was an enormous console television. It was never watched, but always dusted to perfection. Anchoring the room was a life-size sculpture of a mermaid, her graceful hands and knees balancing the thick glass tabletop. It was always a conversation piece for visitors to Aunt Tee's home.

Aunt Tee was married to a man named Ira Johnson. He was a tall, handsome, red-skinned man with big, beautiful hands. They were thick and calloused, but always looked supple, like they had just been washed. He kept his nails clean and cut very low. I remember always wanting to touch his hands to see if they felt as lovely as they looked. He was a practical man who worked construction. He saved enough money to build a fine house for Aunt Tee with her own custom-made walk-in closet to house all the beautiful things he had given her.

Uncle Ira was a wonderful man in many ways, a good father and a great provider. He didn't drink or smoke. He was a homebody, was never unfaithful, and gave Aunt Tee whatever she wanted. But he was strange in other ways. Uncle Ira never smiled, at least not in my presence. I secretly nicknamed him Stone Face, because every time I saw him he was expressionless. And he was a creature of habit. He ate pinto beans with ham hocks and cornbread every single day. It didn't matter what else Aunt Tee cooked, she had to have his pot of beans simmering on the stove when he got home from work.

He was a man of few words, at least when I was around, and I was almost certain he didn't believe in God. He would bring her to church every Sunday, but refused to come in. He'd sit in the car. It didn't matter what the weather conditions were or how long the church service was, he'd wait patiently for her. He didn't turn on the radio and would never fall asleep. Sometimes I'd pretend to go to the bathroom and slip outside just to see what he was doing or if he'd at least gone to run an errand. It was always the same. He'd be sitting there with that granite-like face looking straight ahead. Aunt Tee was a devout Christian without being fanatical, and not just on Sunday but every day of the week. She didn't just talk it, she lived it. Seemed like to me, with all that Jesus, some of it should have rubbed off on him.

He scarcely tolerated other people, but he treated Aunt Tee like a queen. He had bought her exquisite furnishings for her living and dining spaces, but he never allowed visitors access to the rooms, and there was no sitting on the furniture whatsoever. Guests to Aunt Tee's home could walk past and peer into the two rooms, but there was an unspoken rule that those areas were strictly off limits. When Aunt Tee did hair on Saturdays, her customers were relegated to the kitchen and basement areas, and never were they to use the upstairs bathroom.

It was a Thursday, and Daddy had dropped me off at Aunt Tee's after school to get my hair done. Uncle Ira and Tobby were out getting groceries. Aunt Tee had pressed half my head and had taken a break to make a long distance phone call. I quickly ran to the bathroom to see the progression of my transformation. One side of my head was a tiny afro, and the other side was smooth and silky. I smiled to myself as I sprang down the stairs heading back to the kitchen. When I got to the bottom of the steps, I lingered, just taking in the two outlawed rooms. I glanced up the stairs. Aunt Tee was deep in conversation with the door closed. I'd always wanted to know what it would feel like to be inside the museum-like rooms, to touch the mermaid under the glass, to feel the texture of the stone on the giant lamps, to feel the lushness of the sofa.

I stepped one foot into the living room and then the other. I felt a tingle shoot through my body. It was like walking into a forbidden chamber filled with treasures. I sat on the floor next to the mermaid trying to mimic her graceful pose. I ran my fingers along the fine-looking console TV. The china cabinet was a work of art that safeguarded gold-rimmed tableware and crystal glasses. Finally, I sat on the sofa. It didn't feel lush at all. The plastic covers were hard, noisy, and slippery. I put my feet up, and stretched out, trying to find something comfortable about this beautiful piece of furniture. I was wriggling and writhing when I heard the key turning in the front door. I sat up at once only to face Uncle Ira with Tobby and grocery bags in tow. He eyeballed me with a look of loathing. He set the bags down and began walking towards me. I could feel pools of sweat gathering between me and the plastic-covered sofa.

He approached me, and without saying a word, walked right past me and turned on the console TV. "It is a sad day for all Americans," the anchorman said. "Dr. Martin Luther King is dead." King had been shot, shamelessly gunned down while standing on a balcony at the Lorraine Motel in Memphis. Until that day, I didn't know much about Dr. King, but the next several hours would unfold to the world his extraordinary life, painted in vivid colors: A prolific leader, and a giant among men who had honorably led the Civil Rights Movement, he left behind a wife, four children, and a grieving nation. The news reporter imploringly urged all citizens to stay inside because of rioting and looting. We were in a national state of emergency. I'll never forget the images of Black people being beaten and handcuffed and hauled away in paddy wagons. And the hauntingly prophetic words Dr. King had spoken just the night before shook us all to the core as the speech played again and again throughout the broadcast. Aunt Tee appeared from her room and nestled next to me on the couch. And one by one family members and neighbors arrived in silence. This room that had been a kind of shrine was now a gathering place for family and community tearfully huddling in front of the television, mourning our fallen leader.

CHAPTER FIVE

Spring Awakening

FACING FEARS & CLIMBING MOUNTAINS

The Linwood Terrace complex housed spacious one-, two-, and three-bedroom apartments. We lived rent-free in one of the three-bedrooms because Daddy was the resident super. It was a rare spring evening, warm and balmy. Unprecedented sultry weather had graced the region that day. As night began to fall, Sylvia and I sat on the stoop and watched the neighborhood sashay by and the day scamper off into the sunset.

There had been talk of a new family moving into the complex, a single mother and her teenage son. His name was Anthony Tonario. His name alone intrigued me. I mean, what kind of name was Tonario? There were the usual suspects—Washington, Johnson, Jackson, even Hillard—but Tonario? So, I couldn't wait to put a face with this name. The evening was vibrating with activity: cars honking, bicycles whirring by, a softball game, and girls jumping double-dutch across the street. And lurking on the periphery was Anthony Tonario. As he approached us on the stoop, it's as if everything started going in slow motion, especially Anthony. He was tall and gangly, of a fair complexion, with a burst of curly brown hair. He had the smoothest skin and a smile that needed braces. And as soon as he opened his mouth to speak, I was completely besotted.

Three weeks after that, I got my first period. I thought I was dying! I came home from school and barricaded myself in my room until Mama came home. When she arrived, I fell into her arms, hysterical. I was afraid to tell her that I was dying and bleeding from my private place. Filled with foreboding, I composed myself enough to tell her of my impending fate. She laughed and held my tear-stained face in her hands and said, "Oh, chile, it's perfectly normal. You're becoming a woman. It's about this time that all young girls begin having a monthly period, where their bodies discharge blood, marking their transition from girlhood to womanhood." After she calmed me with her gentle tone and some maternal wisdom, she recited a monologue about how easily I could now become pregnant and that sex should be saved until after marriage. She then disappeared into her room and returned with a blue box of Kotex sanitary pads. She gave me a brief tutorial on how to use them, and I reluctantly retreated to the bathroom.

Over the next six months, unbeknownst to my parents, Anthony and I were inseparable. Whenever we were together, my pure human instinct was to kiss him. And ohhh, did we kiss! Endlessly. Anthony was my sexual awakening. We lived in a first floor apartment, and many nights after my parents were asleep I would slip out of my bedroom window to breathlessly make out with Anthony. His mother went out of town on business for a week, and for seven splendid nights Anthony and I played house in their two-bedroom apartment. He'd cook, and I'd wash dishes. He'd play music from his mother's record collection: B.B. King, The Jackson Five, The Temptations. And we'd always wind up in his bed making out till the wee hours. Looking back, I think that was probably one of the best times of my life: young . . . carefree . . . finding love. Anthony and I constantly made out, but we never had sex. I was too afraid. Mama's soliloquy about saving myself for marriage reverberated in my head whenever my virginity was in danger of being compromised.

After six months of living in Linwood Terrace, Miss Tonario's job transferred her to their headquarters in Lansing, Michigan. I was devastated. We had three weeks to say goodbye, and our time was bittersweet. I slipped out of my bedroom window every night for three weeks. And our last night together, we clung to each other till just before daybreak. Tearfully we kissed as he delivered me back to my window, promising to write often. I never heard from him again.

I was in my final year at Garrett A. Morgan. I would be going to high school in the fall. I wasn't in Ms. Brown's class anymore, but she still enlisted my help with her bulletin boards. And she had recommended me to be the soloist for graduation.

I was on my way to an early morning rehearsal that day. I was running late, so I cut through the alley on my way to school. As I got to the center of the alley, a boy appeared out of nowhere. I recognized him, and my breath caught in my chest. The air changed and got thicker as he came closer and blocked my way. His name was Larry Bates. He belonged to a huge family of males who were notorious gang members.

"Where you goin'"? he asked.

"On my way to school." I whispered, trying to find my breath.

"It's kinda early to be goin' to school," he said.

"I'm on my way to a rehearsal for graduation."

I made a step to leave, but once again he blocked my way. My heart was beating so frantically, I could feel it in the back of my throat. His eyes were beady and black, almost devoid of any white. His skin was black, real black, and he had eczema on his face and hands. "Come go with me, just for a few minutes. I'll make sure you get to your rehearsal on time."

I shook my head no, unable to get the word out.

"I won't hurt you, I promise."

I started to cry. That's when he became agitated and told me emphatically, "Shut up"! But I couldn't stop crying. He picked up a bottle and smashed it on the ground and held the razor-sharp edge to my throat. I choked back the tears, and the sound caught in my chest. He led me to an abandoned garage. Inside was an old chaise longue. He instructed me to lie down on it. Reluctantly I did so. He cautiously put the bottle down and slowly reached under my dress to remove my panties.

At that moment, something clicked in my head. I refused cry. I clenched my teeth, and steeled myself for what was about to happen. And I silently began to pray, "Our Father, who art in heaven, hallowed be thy name. Thy kingdom come, thy will be done, on earth as it is in heaven. Give us this day our daily bread, and forgive us our trespasses, as we forgive those who trespass against us. And lead us not into temptation, but deliver us from evil. For thine is the kingdom and the power and the glory forever. Amen."

He unbuckled his belt, and his pants hit the concrete floor with a thud. As he began to pull his underwear down, I shut my eyes. I didn't want to see. He climbed on top of me fully clothed from the waist up. He smelled musty and dirty. He also smelled like menthol—probably an ointment for that unsightly eczema. As he lowered his body onto mine, I braced myself for the unthinkable. When he laid his member on my pelvis, I was completely bewildered. It was flaccid. And it stayed that way. He humped and gyrated for about ten minutes straight. But his penis never got hard.

Finally, I said to myself, "Make sounds like you're enjoying it; maybe he'll stop." I began to faintly moan and sigh. He continued for about a minute and suddenly got up, out of breath.

As he stood there in front of me, I allowed myself to look at it. It was black, and limp, and repulsive. He put his pants back on and handed me my underwear. He told me, "Never, ever tell a soul, or you'll be sorry." It was a threat. And I took him at his word. We left the dilapidated garage and went our separate ways.

I arrived late to school and had to go to the office to get a pass for class. The office administrator could see that I had been crying, and asked me what was wrong. "Nothing," I said. She guardedly gave me the pass and sent me off to homeroom. I was a zombie that day. He hadn't physically raped me, but emotionally he certainly had. I was too afraid of what he and/or his brothers might do. So, I never told anyone. I was well into my thirties when I made the connection between that incident and my innate aversion to dating dark-skinned men. When I think back on the awful incident, I know God answered my prayer that day.

The weeks leading up to graduation brought both joy and anxiety. There were parties and finals, rehearsals and shopping for the perfect graduation dress. Mrs. Evans, the music teacher, gave me three songs to choose from. I ultimately chose "The Way We Were." I had been practicing day in and day out, and I knew the song irrefutably, but I was terrified to sing in front of people. My stage fright was palpable. I was used to singing background, and I enjoyed it immensely because I had a great ear for harmonies. I had never been a soloist. I never wanted to be the person down front leading the choir.

I remember lamenting to Daddy about not being sure if I could sing in front of all those people. "You can do it." He'd say. "The way to conquer your fear is to face it head on. The more you do it, the easier it'll become. You don't want any regrets. You wanna be able to look back at the day and say, I got to that mountain and I climbed it. You don't wanna look back and think to yourself, 'What if?'"

All that week, I kept repeating Daddy's words to myself like a mantra, "You can do it. . . . Face your fears. . . . Climb that mountain. . . . You can do it. . . . Face your fears. . . . Climb that mountain." It was working. I was starting to feel more confident about my solo debut. The anxiety began to give way to excitement.

We were in homeroom reciting the Pledge of Allegiance—"I pledge allegiance to the flag of the United States of America and to the republic for which it stands, one nation under God. . . ."— when suddenly an announcement came over the intercom from the principal: "Faculty and students, it is with great sadness that I inform you of the passing of one of our beloved teachers, Ms. Ann Brown." I felt like I had just been kicked in the stomach. There were gasps and shrieks and students starting to sob. "She had a heart attack in her home last night. That's all I know right now. Once funeral arrangements are made, I will pass those details on to you."

Funeral arrangements . . . Ms. Brown . . . I couldn't believe it. It didn't seem real. I felt like I was daydreaming, like someone would just snap their fingers and jar me out of my reverie. Then I heard someone crying uncontrollably. Suddenly, Mrs. Williams, the homeroom teacher, took me in her arms and began to console me. It was me who was crying hysterically. She led me to the office of the nurse, who gave me two aspirin and a cold compress for my head.

At home that night I asked Mama, "Why did Ms. Brown have to die?"

She tried to make sense of it all. "We have to trust that God knows what he's doing. We loved her, but God loved her best."

The funeral was set for Friday, the day before graduation. It was decided that her service would be held in the school's gymnasium because it was big enough to accommodate her colleagues throughout the Board of Education. I didn't want to go. I didn't want to see her like that, cold and lifeless. Funerals—they were so eerie and macabre. But I had to go. I had to say goodbye.

The gymnasium was a sea of students and teachers paying final respects to one of Chicago's finest educators. Garrett A. Morgan's choir sang, its marching band gave an honorable tribute, and the principal gave the eulogy. Then her body would lie in state for the next six hours for those who'd come to say farewell. Her casket sat surrounded by hundreds of multicolored flowers.

I got in the long line of people to view her body. I could feel my breath getting shorter the closer I got. When I finally made it to the front to see her, I felt a calm come over me. She didn't look scary or macabre at all. She looked peaceful and pretty in her royal blue suit. She looked like she was sleeping. I stood there for what seemed like the longest time studying her face. I didn't ever want to forget it. I would miss her terribly. And wherever she was, I hoped she was looking down and knew how much I loved her, how much she'd touched my life.

Despite the sadness of the previous day, graduation day was exhilarating. Daddy made a breakfast feast which we devoured straightaway. We took lots of pictures in front of the school, and then I scurried to join the other graduates who were beginning to process into the gymnasium. The decorations were so festive; you'd never know a body had been lying in state there twelve hours before. While the valedictorian was delivering his speech, I was going over the song in my head. I took three deep breaths, "You can do it. . . . Face your fears. . . . Climb that mountain." As he finished and took his seat, I thought about Ms. Brown. How I wished she could be there. I knew she'd be proud of me.

The pianist began to play the introduction, and I approached the podium. I looked out and saw Mama and Daddy beaming with pride, and I just began to sing: "Memories light the corners of my mind, misty water-colored memories of the way we were. . . ." How poignant those words were now! When I finished, I took my seat to a rousing standing ovation and not a dry eye in the building. It was an appropriate send-off for the graduates and a lasting tribute to our beloved Ann Brown. R.I.P.

CHAPTER SIX

Aunt Sadie

NO LESS THAN SPIRITUAL

She considereth a field, and buyeth it:
with the fruit of her hands she planteth a vineyard.

PROVERBS 31: 16

Aunt Sadie was the oldest of Mama's siblings. She was bossy and cantankerous, with a deep throaty voice like a man's. She wasn't a pretty woman, but she had a way about her that was alluring. There was no artifice to her, and she had the most beautiful caramel skin I'd ever seen. It felt like silk to the touch. Even well into her sixties, her skin was flawless from head to toe—not one wrinkle, mark, or discoloration. And she had a full head of striking white hair.

She was born Sadie Rose. At ten pounds and nine ounces, she was the biggest baby born to Bertha (Big Mama) and Samuel (Big Papa) Whitlock. She was also a breech birth and had to be delivered by caesarean section. Growing up, Mama said she was a plain-faced tomboy that blossomed into a very desirable woman. Besides her voluptuous curves, she also had something that literally made men swoon—a pair of big, gorgeous legs. She was blessed with small feet and beautifully defined ankles and calves. Each leg was smooth and graceful in shape, and jiggled ever so slightly when she walked.

Aunt Sadie was well aware of her affect on men and used it to her advantage. She had dozens of male suitors and plenty money in the bank when she finally married at the age of thirty-three. She wed a man named Otha Simmons and bore him two sons, Otha Jr. and Gilbert Earl.

Mama said from the beginning, there was something about Otha that just didn't feel right. But he spoke with a charisma and a bravado that swept Aunt Sadie off her feet. He was different from all the other men she took up with. He didn't just talk the talk, but he walked the walk. He'd say, "I'll call," and he always did. When he said, "Baby, I ain't got no wife," it was the absolute truth. He was handsome, intelligent, and there was something a little dangerous about him. He deliberately planned out every date to make it a memorable event, like he was purposefully trying to outdo the last. He enticed her with weekend getaways and concerts and bonfires on the beach. This man knew how to woo a woman, and Aunt Sadie had met her match.

He was a big, burly man with an infectious laugh and a sugary smile. He cajoled her and sweet talked her, and he knew how to make up after a quarrel. He loved her like no other man had and to a fault. It was that crazy kind of love. That "If I can't have you, nobody else will" kind of love.

Otha was jealous beyond belief. They didn't argue about the kids, in-laws, money, or the lack thereof. They argued about her alleged, constant infidelity. Otha was completely obsessed with the idea that she was unfaithful. The first time he hit her was after a dinner party where he accused her of being flirtatious with the husband of a co-worker. They argued on the way to the car, and, just as she slid into the passenger side, he backhanded her so hard she immediately saw stars. And then, just as quickly, she saw red, literally. Blood was gushing from the gash in his face she had made with the keys in her hand.

Mama said Aunt Sadie sported a bruised cheek on her wedding day that was flawlessly hidden under makeup. But Sadie Rose was no shrinking violet. Otha walked with an unmistakable limp down the aisle. After three years of volatile cohabitation and countless police interventions, Aunt Sadie neatly packed her husband's bags and set them orderly outside the front door. She loved him, but she had enough. Otha had to go. When he got home from work that night, two men (who handled a special kind of law enforcement) were on hand to make sure he did just that.

Aunt Sadie was a passionate woman who was fiercely independent. She lived on the first floor of a two-flat on Throop Street on the south side of Chicago. Mama said she purchased it after Otha left, with money he never knew she had. It was a light brown frame structure, with manicured bushes and a lush green lawn. From my first recollection of her 'til the day she died she lived her life exactly the way she wanted, by her own principles, in a lovely home, and unapologetically without a man.

Although Aunt Sadie was gruff and seemed to bark when she talked, she was like a centrifugal force. You were just drawn in. Not only was she full of wisdom and knowledge, but she was bodacious and fun, and there was a subtle sensuality about her. But the thing I found most intriguing was her extraordinary sense of self. She also possessed that unmistakable mother-wit. And I just loved being in her presence.

Sometimes Mama would let me spend the night, and Aunt Sadie would wash and press my hair. The experience was different than getting my hair done at Aunt Tee's. The process seemed like something just short of torture because Aunt Sadie was rough. (Mama called her heavy-handed.) She would wash my hair three times, and to make sure my scalp was clean she'd use a wide-toothed comb during the third wash to scrub away anything her fingertips may have missed. Then she'd part my hair (which is now a tightly curled afro) into four sections. She would make four braids and let them air dry overnight.

The next morning she'd get up and make us a scrumptious breakfast in her small, neat kitchen. I loved to watch her cook. And as she cooked, she'd hum—mostly smoky blues and old ditties in low, rich tones that touched me in ways I couldn't explain. I'd listen and watch while she'd make biscuits from scratch. She'd let me knead the dough and form it into little balls for baking. She'd cook bacon and salt pork, buttery grits, scrambled eggs, and homemade pear preserves.

After our morning feast, I'd wash the breakfast dishes. Once the kitchen was clean, It was time for the next phase of hair business—the pressing. I'd sit in a chair near the stove, and Aunt Sadie would take down one section of hair at a time, put a little oil on it and comb it through. I was so tender-headed, combing through my course, thick hair in its raw state was oh so painful. And although the process of a good pressing was no laughing matter, the end result was sheer bliss. Aunt Sadie would remove the straightening comb from the fire and set it on a towel for a few seconds to cool. If it was still too hot, she'd blow on it a little, and little puffs of smoke would billow through the room. And as she brought the hot comb closer to my scalp, I could feel the heat tickling the back of my neck. And the closer the comb came, the closer my head would instinctively move to the floor. Aunt Sadie would fuss, "Child, you gone make me burn you! Sit still. Relax your shoulders. Hold your ear." It was hard to sit still with a piece of hot iron constantly coming at your head. I'd be so physically exhausted, I always had to take a nap when we were done.

But my favorite part of the whole process came after Aunt Sadie had pressed the last section of hair and turned off the stove. She would part my hair in the smallest of sections from front to back and carefully oil my scalp with a special salve she kept in the refrigerator. That cool ointment on my still warm scalp was so completely soothing that something about it still resonates deep in my soul. Just the feeling of her fingertips and that cool salve running from the front of my head to the nape of my neck was something no less than spiritual. Then she'd comb out my hair and style it however I wanted, which was usually two ponytails. It was always amazing to see the transformation from the little puff of hair to two smooth braids that hung well past my shoulders.

Aunt Sadie owned two pieces of rental property that sustained her well enough that she never had to work. She and her boys were well taken care of. In raising them, she never wanted them to be idle, so she enrolled them in Little League, basketball, tap, and piano. It was clear early on that Gilbert Earl was the athlete, while Otha Jr. embraced his artistic side. He loved to perform, and he excelled in tap and piano. He had a flair about him that made the other boys take notice and poke fun. Even Gilbert Earl began to treat him differently.

A week before I started high school, Daddy lost his job as super of the residential building where we lived. Hence, we lost our apartment and had to move. Aunt Sadie offered us the three-bedroom flat above her. She said she'd be glad for the company since Gilbert Earl was married with children and Otha Jr. now spent very little time at home. She also told us that Otha Jr. was different these days, but to pay him no mind because he was going through a phase.

We had been in the apartment about a week when all hell broke loose. Daddy arrived home from work late one night in a state of what seemed like sheer panic. He pulled Mama into the front room. "Em, we ain't gone be able to stay here. That boy done lost his mind! He's a sissy. And he's a sissy in the worst kinda way. I just ran into that boy comin' up the stairs. At first, I didn't even know who he was. That boy had on a sequined mini-dress and high-heeled shoes, a long curly wig, and had his face painted up like he was goin' to a clown show. He told me, 'I don't go by Otha anymore, I prefer to be called CeCe.'"

By this time, all us kids had overheard the news and made our way into the living room. Just then, Daddy pointed to the front window. Crossing the street was Otha (CeCe) in stockings and heels. The mini-dress sparkled prettily under the glow of the street lights. And as he swished from side to side, the hemline of his tiny shimmering dress danced playfully just below his butt cheeks. His hand went up to tuck the hair behind one ear, and he flung the long curls over his shoulder. And with his long legs, he walked out of sight like a gazelle, swinging his matching sequined handbag.

Over the next several months, before Hazel left for college, we lived for CeCe sightings. Sometimes we wouldn't see him for days at a time, and when we did, it was always late at night as he left the house (to do whatever it was he did dressed like that). After Hazel left for college, I began spending more time at Aunt Sadie's. Daddy and the boys never darkened her door for fear of running into CeCe. But Mama and I were frequent visitors at Aunt Sadie's kitchen table. She certainly didn't approve of her son's lifestyle, and it was understood that whatever he did in the streets was to stay there. It was never to be brought into her home.

The Otha I remembered as a child long since had been gone. And getting to know CeCe was fascinating to me. She was the same chatty person he had been, just more so. Otha's voice was deep, so CeCe affected a voice that was much lighter. It was almost a whisper when she talked. And she gave every "s" great importance and punctuation. She let me watch her apply her makeup one night. The process was captivating. First, she carefully shaved her face and neck and plucked her eyebrows. Then she applied foundation to her face and neck. She smoothed a blue shadow on her eyelids and crowned them with long, lush lashes. She took a dark brown pencil and drew a beautiful arch to each brow. She dusted her cheeks with a rosy blush and pursed her lips to apply a gorgeous matte, red lipstick. Finally, she pulled her hair back and covered it with a tight, black stocking cap and slipped on a long, flowing wig. (She called it her crown.) It was a stunning transformation, but even without close inspection, anyone could tell that she was a he. Her face was long and her pores were deep. And even with all the beautiful makeup, she wasn't pretty. She was much better looking as a man.

A year had passed since we moved into Aunt Sadie's two-flat. Daddy and the boys would occasionally encounter CeCe. She would greet them in her soft, whispery voice, and they would nod a hello. It was a Friday, and I was at the kitchen sink washing dishes when Shane burst through the back door and quickly locked it behind him. Seconds later, there was banging on the other side of the door, and a baritone voice with a seismic rumble yelling, "Open this door, Nigga! Open this damn door! I'm gone beat your ass!"

Mama, Clem Jr., and Ray rushed into the kitchen to see what the matter was. Shane, still out of breath, said, "It's Otha."

Mama said, "You mean CeCe?"

Shane said, "No! I mean Otha! He ain't no woman! And I'm sick of him whisperin' and sashayin' around here like he is! I told that sissy to get out my face and he wouldn't, so I snatched that wig off his head and threw it across the yard."

The banging continued for about a minute and then we heard weeping. Mama opened the door to find CeCe curled up on the porch sobbing uncontrollably. I helped Mama bring her inside. She seemed so vulnerable and somehow utterly naked. She was truly a pitiful sight as she sat at the kitchen table fully made up, with her beaded dress torn, barefoot, and without her crown. I inwardly wept for CeCe. She was just lonely, hurting, and horribly misunderstood—a human being who only wanted unconditional love and acceptance like anyone else on a quest to find their place in the world.

When things were calm, Aunt Sadie came upstairs to collect her broken son. CeCe moved out of Aunt Sadie's house that following Sunday.

CHAPTER SEVEN

MEANING OF LIFE

In the twilight, in the evening, in the black and dark night:
And behold there met him a woman
with the attire of a harlot, and subtle of heart.
She is loud and stubborn; her feet abide not in her house:
I have peace offerings with me; this day have I paid my vows.

PROVERBS 7:9, 10, 11, 14

Soon Daddy grew weary of the politics at Morning Star and announced that he was leaving to start his own church. They gave us a wonderful send-off. On our last Sunday, the church was bursting with well-wishers and guest choirs. The feast the Church Sisters had prepared was fit for a king. They presented Daddy with a beautiful robe to wear in the new church and, I think, were genuinely sorry to see us go. It was shortly after we left Morning Star we learned that church services were to be held in the garage attached to the back of our house.

It was the summer of 1974 when we finally moved into a house of our own. After years of shabby apartment dwelling and roving from pillar to post, we would now walk on floors that belonged to us. Aunt Sadie's flat had served us well, but Mama was unwavering about getting a home of our own. She and Daddy bought it from an aging Jewish couple. Daddy said he thought they were moving out of the neighborhood because too many Blacks were moving in. It was a spacious five-bedroom, brick house on the southeast side of Chicago near Lake Michigan. It had three bathrooms, a big basement, an ample back yard, and a cozy little kitchen. Mama's eyes danced around each room, contemplating what picture to put here and what chair to place there. I had never seen her happier than the day we moved in. And I was on cloud nine because Sylvia lived around the corner.

A typical Sunday would begin with Daddy teaching Sunday school, followed by devotion and the morning worship service. There was lots of singing, nodding, and swaying. There was tapping, clapping, jerking and holy dancing, and speaking in tongues. Every Sunday some woman would get the Spirit. She would fall out and her dress would fly up, exposing the secrets underneath her clothes. And ushers were always poised with white sheets to quickly cover our blessed sister. It was hard to focus on the service because the Sunday dinner Mama had prepared beforehand would waft through the room and tickle our noses with aromas of the delicious meal that awaited us. We sat with Mama every Sunday and listened to Daddy preach and teach and pray with fervor. He said, "If you lift Jesus up, he will draw the people."

Some of the first members to join the church were Aunt Tee, two elder brothers from Christ Temple Church in Evanston, and Aunt Sky. Aunt Tee had been a long-time member of Haven of Rest Baptist Church. She sat on the Mother's Board, was an accomplished fundraiser, and had plenty money of her own. She also knew how to get a prayer through. Now, Aunt Sky was a recovering alcoholic who smoked two packs of cigarettes a day.

That same year Aunt Sky came to live with us after Uncle Gus died, her common-law husband of seventeen years. Arteriosclerosis claimed his life at the age of fifty-eight. He literally drank himself to death. As a couple they were terrible drunkards, intoxicated with the drink at every family reunion, funeral, wedding, graduation—and . . . we . . . loved . . . them. A family gathering wasn't complete without Aunt Sky and Uncle Gus. They were wonderful storytellers. Together they shared witty proverbs, comic tales, wicked truisms, and outrageous anecdotes. Aunt Sky would literally have us rolling on the floor with her comments, quips, and quick retorts. They were two people who could fill a room with life and laughter, soul mates who had never been apart for more than a day or two.

Aunt Sky's zest for life died the day we buried Uncle Gus. And she also buried her love and need for the drink. She moved into the basement, which was cold and dark and spookier than anything I'd seen on TV. There were huge spiders and cobwebs and creaky doors that led to dark, musty storage rooms, and sounds coming from the boiler room that likened a woman's muffled screams. Sometimes we'd play hide and seek, and send the new kid to hide in the basement. We'd fall out laughing when we'd hear their frantic feet barreling up the stairs, out of breath, saying, "There's somethin' down there! There's somethin' down there!"

Three days after Aunt Sky moved in, I came home from school and heard faint music coming from the basement. I quietly opened the door so I could hear the music better. It was slow and bluesy, and I smiled as the glorious music and the smell of fried chicken filled the staircase. I proceeded down the stairs to peek through one of three small windows on the landing. As I did, I was astonished by what I saw. The old dirty windows had been cleaned to a sparkle and were now dressed with pretty, white lace curtains, tied back so the sun shone in. Pushed up against one wall was an old comfortable couch. Opposite it were two cozy chairs and a small round table, topped with a crisp white doily and some fresh flowers from the back yard. She had positioned her bed against the back wall and dressed it in starched white linens and the colorful quilt Big Mama had made. The dull, dingy floor had been mopped and waxed to a high shine. And several throw rugs had been tossed about. No longer was it dark, cold, and scary, but warm and homey, and eventually it became my favorite place to be.

Aunt Sky turned the creepy boiler room into her food pantry. She painted it eggshell white and put Crisco on the rusty parts of the boiler to stop the ear-piercing sounds it made, that sometimes kept me awake nights. She also made some improvements in the garage where Daddy held Sunday church service. She made seat cushions for the hard chairs, and, since there was no air conditioning, she had the neighborhood funeral parlor donate hand fans. She specified that they send the ones with a picture of Dr. Martin Luther King Jr. on the front. And over each window she put a plastic overlay that resembled stained glass.

Aunt Sky wasn't a Christian, but Mama and Daddy persuaded her to join the church. They were firm believers in the power of prayer. Aunt Sky was no longer the alcoholic I had known all my life, but she was still a chain smoker, and she loved the blues. Both were huge sins in Daddy's eyes. Every Sunday he'd call for those who wanted to get right with God or who needed healing to come down front for prayer. And every Sunday Aunt Sky would walk to the altar and Daddy would lay hands on her, along with Mama, Aunt Tee, and the other elders, and they would ardently pray God's blessings over her. And each time it was the same. The elders would pray themselves happy, and Aunt Sky would leave the circle nonplussed by it all. This particular Sunday, when Daddy made the altar call, she went as she had many times before. But this time when Daddy and the elders laid hands on her and began to pray, something amazing happened. Her whole body began to shake. She raised her hands as if surrendering to something or someone. She began to weep. And as I watched in awe, I remember her saying over and over again, "Yes, Lord. Yes, Lord. Yes, Lord." That day was the liberation of Aunt Sky. Not only was she born again spiritually, but mentally and physically.

Over the next few months, the life that seemed to be buried with Uncle Gus began slowly reemerging. The distinct, raucous laughter, the quick wit and tales of old we'd missed so much began to fall effortlessly from her lips. She even looked different. The furrow in her brow seemed somehow smoothed. The toll that years of drinking and hard living had taken now didn't seem so evident on her face. She had a new lease on life and a love for all things Christian. She immersed herself in the Bible and became a Sunday school teacher. Daddy enjoyed taking her along when we went church visiting. She was his Amen Corner all by herself. There was a palpable joy about her. In church, we cherished the fact that she clapped, stomped, and sang louder than everyone else. She seemed to do everything with such unbridled passion. We even loved her laughter. She would throw her head back, and the sound was rich, deep, and musical. It was a sound you just loved to hear. It was the laughter of a woman who had tapped into the meaning of life.

I had enrolled in South Shore, and Sylvia went to Carver High. Every day we couldn't wait to get home and exchange stories about who was cute and who we had crushes on, our favorite teachers, and who the mean girls were. I told Sylvia about a girl I met in gym class. Her name was Yolanda Knight. She was absolutely nothing like Sylvia. She was loud, a little crass, and matter-of-fact, but hilarious. She made me laugh incessantly, and I loved that about her. And if South Shore had a best-dressed award to be given, it should have gone to Yolanda. She wore the finest clothes and shoes. She said she and her mom had been in a couple of car accidents and had received two large settlements, so shopping had become their favorite pastime. Yolanda was very popular and, to this day, I'm still not quite sure why she chose to hang out with me. But we were thick as thieves. I began to split my time between her and Sylvia. Yolanda was my buddy at school. But Sylvia was my inimitable BFF. And individually they fed different parts of me.

That day, Yolanda and I decided to go off campus for lunch. Joe's Chicken Shack was a little restaurant down the street from the school. They served hamburgers and hot dogs, polish sausages and the best fried chicken. On our way to Joe's, Yolanda glanced over her shoulder and then revealed a tiny bag from her purse. From the bag she pulled out a reefer.

"Girl! Where'd you get that?" I was now deliberately whispering.

"I got it from my brother." She said. "I thought it might be kinda cool to try it. Oh, come on. It can't be that bad. Everybody does it."

I was skeptical, but eventually gave in. We ducked behind a van in the school parking lot and passed the joint back and forth, smoking it completely. By the time we got to Joe's, it was teeming with its usual lunch crowd. We grabbed a booth in the back and ordered two double cheeseburgers with fries and two vanilla shakes. We were ravenous! By the time the waitress came with our food, I was so mellow, I could have put my head down on the table and taken a nap. But Yolanda was paranoid. She swore the salt and pepper shakers were moving, along with the plastic ketchup and mustard dispensers. An hour would go by before she felt normal enough to go back to class.

We had already missed sixth period, and all the other students were gone from Joe's. So, we started the three-block walk back to school. In the middle of the block, the sky suddenly got dark. A murky cloud seemed to come out of nowhere and hoover above us. Eerily, it seemed to follow us into the next block. Yolanda, who was still slightly paranoid from the reefer said, "Why does it look like that cloud is following us?" Before she could fully finish the phrase, it seemed like the heavens opened up and assailed us with torrential rain and hail. The downpour lasted only about a minute, but it was enough to soak us from head to toe. We were flabbergasted, because the dark cloud quickly gave way to the clearest blue sky. When we arrived at seventh period, we were met with snickers and stares. Nobody believed our story, because the area around the school hadn't received a drop of rain.

I was so uncomfortable in the wet clothes, I went home early. When I got there, Aunt Sky was sitting on the porch. "What happened to you?" She asked. Much as I wanted to, I couldn't lie. I told her everything—about the reefer, the double cheeseburgers, the rain, and the hail. She just bust out laughing. And every time I thought she was finished, she'd bust out laughing again. Finally, she said, "You are special. You can't do what everybody else does. Smokin' reefer ain't for you. And today God let you know that loud and clear." I haven't smoked another reefer to this day.

Over the next twenty-four months, others joined the church, and Aunt Tee raised enough money for a down payment on a building. The new church was a huge, abandoned storefront that hadn't been occupied for years. There was an old bowling alley on the second floor and two smaller storefronts on either side. Mama complained of it being too big and needing too much work. She wanted to purchase a piece of property that was an existing church. But Daddy was adamant that one storefront could house a restaurant, the other a day care center, and we could eventually refurbish and open the dilapidated bowling alley. Mama wasn't convinced, but she acquiesced and reluctantly supported his vision.

Daddy did all the work himself with occasional help from our next door neighbor, Mr. James, and long-time friend, Chappy Smith. Mr. James was also a minister and a veteran painter by trade with a lot of mouth. He was a great debater of family issues, current events, and church politics. He always boasted of being exceptional at his craft, but his work was generally sloppy, he was rarely on time, and he always wanted his money up front. Chappy Smith was a devoted friend of the family. He was dependable, loved to eat, and drank lots of coffee because he had narcolepsy (or what Daddy called "the sleeping disease"). Sometimes he'd be mid-sentence and helplessly drop off to sleep. His expertise was in plastering, and he was a master at his craft. He could take cracked, peeling, warped, or uneven walls and work miracles. He'd do all the heavy work in the first layer. But when he applied the last layer, it was simply beautiful to watch. It was like watching a great artist at work. And he was an artist. His strokes were light, quick, and graceful. When he was done, the old walls were chalky white but perfectly smooth, like fresh sheets of drywall.

The day we opened Bible Way Church of God in Christ is a day I'll never forget. The Senior Bishop had been invited as keynote speaker, and several guest churches were in attendance. We all worked tirelessly that Saturday before, readying the church for Inauguration Sunday. The smell of sawdust, plaster, and fresh paint was in the air. There were new toilets and lighting fixtures, and old stadium seating had been donated. All of the visitors were greeted and ushered to the left side of the church to be seated, because Daddy hadn't had enough time to bolt down the seating on the right side. Testimonies had gone forth, the choir had sung, and the bishop had just taken the pulpit when it started to storm. Daddy rushed to get a bucket for a leak near the pulpit. Before he could get back, more containers were needed to catch all the rain that was falling in our new church. Daddy quietly instructed the usher to help him get more containers for the leaks. The bishop never stopped preaching.

Distracted by the rain making puddles on the floor, no one noticed Chappy Smith come in and sit in the first row of the unsecured seating on the right. There was good old Chappy, just sitting there. He adjusted a bit, then reached down to get his Bible from his briefcase and sat back, hard. The first row tipped back, and one by one like dominoes each row crashed into the next. After a stunned silence, several men instinctively leapt to help Chappy and to right the stadium seats. When Chappy stumbled a bit, but nodded that he was OK, we fell out laughing—me, Hazel, Clem Jr., Shane, baby brother Ray, and cousin Tobby. The bishop cracked a joke, finished his sermon, and took up a special collection for immediate roof repairs. Daddy later scolded us for setting a bad example in the face of company. But he knew it didn't take much to crack us up. And he knew Tobby was always the ring leader.

Tobby was Aunt Tee's son, who was a self-taught pianist. He couldn't play a note if you gave him sheet music, but if you sang it, he could play it. If you began a cappella, he could quickly find your key and render beautiful accompaniment. Tobby was silly, foolish even. And Daddy was well aware of it. But he was a huge asset to our church. So Daddy looked past his immaturity and embraced his extraordinary talent. Not only did Tobby write, play, and conduct us when we sang, but he could sing—as the old folks would say—"until heaven got the news." It gave Daddy great joy to hear us sing. He would take us with him when he had to preach at other churches. And right before his sermon he'd proudly say, "I'd like to call on my choir for an A and B selection." He'd chide us in the car beforehand to mind our manners. He'd say, "I don't care what happens tonight, don't y'all embarrass me. Don't act a fool." But if something funny happened we honestly could not help ourselves.

This particular Sunday we were visiting a church, and the minister preached with lots of growling and spitting and clearing of his throat. He wiped his mouth and, unbeknownst to him, left a big wad of mucus in his beard. And it stayed there for the duration of his sermon. I only had to make eye contact with Tobby and I was no good until the benediction. If one got tickled, we all got tickled. It was infectious. And we dared not laugh out loud or even snicker, or we'd call more attention to ourselves. But holding it in made it ten times funnier. Tears swelled in our eyes, and our shoulders shook uncontrollably. Even Aunt Sky helplessly joined in the laughter. On the way home Daddy didn't scold us much. He saw the mucus too and thought to himself, "For the love of God, why doesn't the man use his handkerchief?" We laughed all the way home.

CHAPTER EIGHT

Aunt Mae

PEACE & RESOLVE

Strength and honor are her clothing;
and she shall rejoice in the time to come.

PROVERBS 31: 25

Aunt Mae was Mama's godsister, whose own mother had died at birth, so Big Mama and Big Papa raised her as their own. Etta Mae Whitlock wed Mr. Daniel Frank Jamison on her eighteenth birthday. After giving birth to their first child, she bore him thirteen more children. Of all the sisters, Aunt Mae was the smallest. She was tiny. She stood about four feet eight inches tall, and was very petite. Everything about her was diminutive—her voice, her hands and feet, even her features. She and Daniel had migrated north, and were living with twelve of their children in a cramped, three-bedroom apartment on Chicago's west side. And two of those children now had children of their own.

As a young girl, I remember going to Aunt Mae's on holidays like Memorial Day or the Fourth of July. Shane and I would always ask, "Mama, can we go over Aunt Mae 'n Nem house?" We referred to them as "Aunt Mae and them" because she had too many children to call them all by name. Visiting them was always pure pleasure because there were so many kids to play with just from Aunt Mae's household alone. And we'd always go home happy, worn out, and bandaged up from the cuts and scrapes we got from romping in the concrete play lot.

There were five boys and seven girls. The girls were Vivian, Pauline, Marilyn, Eva, Barbara, JoAnne, and Claudette. The boys were Clifford, Danny Jr., Robert, James, and Samuel who was born developmentally disabled. Two of Aunt Mae's children were twins and had died at birth.

Every room in Aunt Mae's apartment was small and crammed with too much furniture. I remember always feeling claustrophobic just entering the front door. And the longer I stayed, the smaller the rooms became. The living room housed three worn, mismatched couches that served as sleepers for three of the boys at bedtime. The doors to the bedrooms were kept closed to hide the piles of dirty clothes, trash, and utter chaos. The bathroom was odorous and moist because the tub's hot water faucet didn't shut off completely. And there were roaches everywhere! So, I didn't eat Aunt Mae's cooking. Just the sight of roaches in the kitchen literally made me sick to my stomach. I always envisioned some of the tiny creepy-crawlers being cooked in with the food.

Aunt Mae worked tirelessly. And she wore a certain weary look on her face. When Aunt Mae wasn't cooking or cleaning, she was caring for her two grandchildren. Not only were their mamas (Barbara and JoAnne) late sleepers, they were also downright lazy. They ran the streets at night, and Aunt Mae granted them the luxury of sleeping well into the afternoon. But they gave Aunt Mae a portion of their welfare checks. Mama said it was a trade-off Aunt Mae wearily agreed to before the death of her husband. Every one of Aunt Mae's children lacked something Mama called "gumption." And she always over-enunciated the word. I didn't know what it meant, but I loved how the word sounded coming out of her mouth.

Sometimes I'd overhear Mama talking about Aunt Mae's late husband. She'd say, "Honey, Daniel Jamison was a piece o' man."

But Aunt Mae would always reply, "Chile, a piece o' man is better than no man at all."

Everything I knew about Daniel Jamison, I learned by eavesdropping on private conversations. Daniel Frank Jamison was a seasoned liar and a notorious womanizer. He was a serial philanderer who bed a never-ending pageant of voracious women. He was a whore to the bone. Mama said when Aunt Mae met him, he didn't have a pot to pee in or a window to throw it out of. He felt he was God's gift to women, and he generously gave of himself again and again. She said he was the kind of man who could talk all underneath a woman's clothes in such a way that when he finished, she was flattered, never offended. He was a tall, thin man, with dangerously good looks. Aunt Sky said he was pretty as a panther. Not only was he satisfying to look at, he knew how to spin words like silk. She said he was a gorgeous black man, said he was black as a patent leather shoe, said he was so black he sweat chocolate. And every one of Aunt Mae's children was blessed with their father's smooth, shadowy complexion.

Daniel Jamison lived a frivolous life and had no real occupation, but he was never without money. He was kept by the women he philandered around with. They dressed him in fine clothes and flashy jewelry. He'd stay out for days at a time. Upon his return, Aunt Mae would threaten to put him out, but he was a master at sweet-talking and side-stepping. After cajoling her, he'd give her money for the bills and the kids, and she'd give in. He was shamelessly unfaithful, but what could she do? She was trapped. She had no college education, no trade—only him and all those mouths to feed. How cruel fate was!

I heard someone say, "The blues ain't nothin' but a good woman feelin' bad." And Aunt Mae was a good woman who had the sho-nuff blues. And the misery that flickered across her face told a story all its own, like she was silently screaming. Visibly, she was in pain—a woman wounded on the inside, stretched too thin, and yearning for peace. She would hear of her husband's womanizing from neighbors, church members, and occasionally her own children. It was widely rumored that he had been seeing a woman who lived at 40th and Drexel, and he was about to be a father yet again. One bitter morning in December, Aunt Mae got a call informing her that Daniel was dead. He had been found in his car with a bullet in his head. The car was parked in front of a brownstone at 4055 South Drexel.

The ironies of life's circumstances are mysterious. Aunt Mae wasn't a member of Bible Way and Daniel Jamison had unquestionably lived a hellish life, but Daddy opened the doors of our church for his home going. Aunt Mae's demeanor was serene, as she sat looking splendid in all white, flanked on either side by her children. She never approached his coffin, but watched each one of her children walk up and offer a personal goodbye to their father. She was stoic. Aunt Mae sat like stone as the tearful mistress, clad in all black, approached the casket to peruse Daniel's now lifeless body. On her hip bounced a precious baby boy with soft tufts of curly brown hair, Daniel Jamison's arresting eyes, and that beautiful black skin. Aunt Mae never shed a tear. The weariness that Aunt Mae had worn on her face was replaced with what Mama described as that of peace and resolve.

The police never solved the mystery of who killed Daniel Jamison. And the family never discussed it openly, but it was whispered that it was Aunt Mae who pulled the trigger.

A week after she buried her husband, Aunt Mae called a family meeting. At first it seemed more like a party, because there was food and drink and music, and we were all in attendance. Just as the party reached a fevered pitch, Aunt Mae called us all to order: "I buried my husband last week. Put him in the ground. And as I watched them lower his body into the earth, I thought to myself, 'Thank ya, Jesus! There is a God!'" And a hush fell over the room.

"Everybody in this room knows that Daniel Frank Jamison was a trifling, good-for-nothin', lyin', sweet-talkin' whore! For the past twenty-six years that man literally sucked the very life out of me.

Never took responsibility as a father or a husband, wouldn't keep a job. He never once asked me what I wanted out of life. He didn't care. He just wanted a soft place to fall when he came in out of the streets. And I gave him that—woman after woman, year after year, baby after baby. And because I had all y'all, I was convinced I needed him. I thought with all these mouths to feed, I couldn't do no better. But God as my witness, a better time is comin'. And that time is in about sixty days. On or before March 15th, Barbara and JoAnne, you and your children will be moving out. So you'll need to start looking for jobs or more government assistance. You will take Vivian, Pauline, and Eva to help with the kids.

"To my girls I say, 'Don't be like me. Don't do what I did. Never let a man take and take and take and give you nothin' in return. And never, ever wrap yourself up so much in a man that you lose you. Love yourselves, I mean really love yourselves, and in simply doing that, you will teach men how to treat you.'

"To my boys I say, 'Your father was a sorry excuse for a man. He was the worst kind of fatherly role model a son could have. And for that I am so sorry. The true measure of a man is not defined by how many women you can bed or how many children you can make. At the end of the day, it is being accountable to yourself, taking responsibility for those children you do father, and honoring the women who give birth to them.' Clifford and Danny, you must also be out by March 15th. You are grown men, and you are old enough to take care of yourselves. The rest of you can stay here until you turn eighteen. And after that you have got to make your own way. Samuel, of course, will always have a place here with me.

"I'm tired, I'm worn out, but I wanna try to reclaim some part of my life back. For years I have lived in my own personal hell, and that's not your fault. But I . . . I cannot continue to take care of you, to cook and fix your plates, and babysit, and wash your clothes, and clean, and clean, and clean until my hands are raw! I have given you so much of me, I am poured out. I have nothing left to give. And allowing you to stay here and not take responsibility for yourselves not only drains me, but it stifles you. It holds you back. And if I don't put a stop to it now, not one of you will amount to anything. And I will not be blamed for that.

"Now, I'm gone fix me a plate of food and then do something I haven't done in a long time. I'm gone take a nap." And with that, she quietly walked out of the room, leaving us to talk amongst ourselves.

That day clearly marked a paradigm shift in the entire Jamison family. That day Aunt Mae began redefining herself and ultimately reordering her life. The March 15th deadline came, and only the children below the age of eighteen remained under her auspices. And Aunt Mae began to clean house. The kids were given chores. An exterminator was called in to debug the house. Every room was completely cleaned out and reorganized with only the furniture needed. With seven of her children now out on their own, it was like a pressure cooker had been, not turned off, but—thank God—turned down. She now had five mouths to feed instead of twelve.

With no real education or trade she turned to her church. Aunt Mae started out cleaning the bathrooms and polishing the pews. After a year, they hired her to be head cook, preparing meals for the less fortunate. It was a job that gave her great satisfaction. Sometimes I would go and help her prepare and organize things in the bustling kitchen. It was hard work. There was a never-ending assembly line of vegetables to be chopped, greens to be cleaned, dough to be kneaded, chicken to be fried, potatoes to be peeled, cakes and pies to be baked, and dishes to be washed.

Once, after an exhausting day in the kitchen, I was so tired, I just wanted to curl up in a fetal position. Aunt Mae said she couldn't tell how tired she was because her feet hurt so badly. So, we took our shoes off and sat with two tall glasses of ice-cold lemonade. We put our feet up on two adjacent chairs. Wiggling my toes around, I asked, "Aunt Mae, would you ever want to do any other kind of work?"

After a moment of contemplation, she said, "Greta, I am paid to do something that gives me great joy. And to have people value the work that I do is the best feeling in the world. I guess . . . I feel needed . . . more importantly, I feel appreciated. Unh unh, I can't imagine myself doing anything else."

Then she said something that I found so simple, yet very profound. She said, "When you figure out what you want to do in life, make sure it's something that you love, 'cause if you do something that you love and somebody pays you to do it, most days it won't feel like work." As we sat luxuriating, drinking lemonade and wiggling our toes, I realized a new, different, better Aunt Mae had emerged. And I wasn't at all sure when the transformation had occurred.

CHAPTER NINE

Saturday Mornin'
FELLOWSHIP

On Saturdays Aunt Tee's beauty shop was open for business. Most of her clients came for a wash, press, and curl, but they also came for the good fellowship. Every Saturday was a social gathering. The women cooked and ate, speechified, told tales, and gossiped. They engaged in some of the freest, most hilarious repartee I've ever witnessed. They talked about everything, from their men, to their children, to church politics, to world issues.

Uncle Ira hated all the cackling and the smell of pressed hair in the house, so he would leave early on Saturday mornings and return after all her clients had gone home. Aunt Tee would finish all her heads by 4:00 p.m. and start his dinner. She was well aware that the aroma of food cooking always over-powered the lingering smell of pressed hair. I secretly cleaned Aunt Tee's house on Saturday mornings and finished well before Uncle Ira was expected home. He thought outside help made other people privy to their personal business. Most Saturdays he'd come home, and the house would be spotless. He'd always give me and Aunt Tee that look of knowing, but said nothing and went on his way. Aunt Tee would give me a wink, and we'd laugh deliciously under our breath.

Aunt Tee and Uncle Ira took in a foster child named Edwin. Mama said he was born with a veil over his face, so he could see spirits and things other people couldn't. He was eight years old and was extremely small for his age. His two front teeth were badly broken and slightly buck. He had a nauseatingly high-pitched voice and sounded eerily like Alvin the Chipmunk. Tobby and I had been a twosome for so long, he was a third wheel. He was weird, and we simply didn't want him around. So we'd hide from Edwin, but he'd always find us. He'd sneak up on us and give us a start by screaming or making a loud noise. He'd throw his head back and laugh, exposing his sharp teeth. Edwin was altogether annoying and a little bit scary.

Once we attended a wake at a funeral home. A long-time friend of Aunt Tee's had passed away. After the service, we also attended a repast for the family in a hall on the premises. We just sat down to eat when Aunt Tee said, "Where's Edwin?" Ray and Hazel went with Tobby to find him. I refused to go. I had seen a dead body in an open casket in another room, and I was sure that there were dead people lying in state all over the place. Moments later they ushered him in and pushed him down in the chair next to me. They were laughing hysterically. They had found him in a room talking to a corpse, saying things like, "Hey, what's your name? Hey, what you doin' in there? Hey you, wake up."

Edwin was also hardheaded, a habitual liar, and very sneaky. Aunt Tee would constantly tell him to stop this or that. He would stop momentarily, then shift his beady eyes her way to ensure she wasn't looking and resume his mischievous deed. He would disobey and misbehave 'til she'd say, "See, your head is hard. I'm gonna tell Ira when he gets home, and you are surely gonna get it." But he was slick, cunning even. He pulled tricks on Aunt Tee he instinctively knew not to try with Uncle Ira. He was an angel whenever Uncle Ira was around. It would be a long time before I found out that Edwin went to school on the short bus.

For the next year it became ritual for me to clean Aunt Tee's house on Saturdays (while Uncle Ira was at work), and she'd pay me $25. I'd spend the night, and Uncle Ira would take us to church on Sunday mornings. I slept in Edwin's room because he had two twin beds. He always woke at the crack of dawn, before anyone else even began to stir. He'd throw small objects like paper clips or hairpins at my head to wake me out of my slumber. Sometimes he'd hit the bed with his fist while making weird noises with his throat, then quickly jump back into his bed.

Once, when I was sleeping, he used his fingers to flick cold water in my face. When I opened my eyes, I saw his jagged teeth smiling down at me. I was so mad, I mostly saw red. Before I knew it, I lunged at him and pinned him to the floor. I was pummeling his forehead with the knuckle of my middle finger. Within seconds I could see a huge knot swelling between his eyebrows. I would surely get in trouble for this. But he had to be taught a lesson. Before I released my grip, through clenched teeth, I threatened, "If you ever hit me with a spitball, paper clip, or anything trying to wake me, if you ever touch my bed or flick water on me or make those idiotic throat noises ever again, I'll bust your head wide open." There was something in his eyes I had never seen before—terror. And with that, I arose triumphant and got back in the bed.

When I awoke again, it was Aunt Tee's voice I heard. "Boy, what happened to your head?" He began to explain to her that I did it. I was in hot water now. Should I tell the truth? Should I make up a lie? My mind was racing. And then I heard Aunt Tee say, "If there's one thing I can't stand, it's a liar. Get outta my face! Ira, this boy's in here telling lies again!" I snickered under the covers. I was exonerated before ever going to trial. I had beaten him down, and no one was the wiser. I emerged from the bedroom victorious. I kissed Aunt Tee good morning and slyly winked at Edwin as I bounced off to wash for breakfast.

Aunt Tee was so busy on Saturdays with all the heads to be done, she needed help with housekeeping. I'd sweep and vacuum, dust, do dishes, and organize. One day I was rearranging her closet. I was just finishing up and shining the full-length mirror when Uncle Ira walked in. He was furious. "We don't need her cleaning our house for us!" He yelled. I couldn't figure out why he didn't like me. Aunt Tee would say, "Aw, baby, it's not that he doesn't like you, it's just his way."

Mama said, "Mean people like your Uncle Ira have to be killed with kindness."

Now, like I said, Uncle Ira was a creature of habit. He took a bath every night before he went to bed. On this particular occasion, I was spending the night. After I took my bath, I had an epiphany: Kill him with kindness. That's what he needs—a simple, random act of kindness. So, after my bath, I washed out the tub and ran it full of hot soapy water. I was proud of myself. I felt warm and fuzzy. I was extending the olive branch. But the fragile limb snapped as he hit the bathroom door once hard and barked, "Come on out of there. It don't take that long to get no bath." After a few moments, I put my ear to the door. When I heard him descending the stairs to the basement, I slipped into Aunt Tee's bedroom to inform her of what I had done. There was still hope. Once he entered the bathroom and saw the warm, sudsy water I'd prepared for him, he'd feel sorry and ashamed of how he had treated me, of how he'd treated me all along. I was in Tobby's room telling him of my good deed when we heard Uncle Ira coming up the stairs. We then stepped out of his room to witness what was about to happen.

As Uncle Ira crossed the threshold of the bathroom Aunt Tee sweetly exclaimed, "Ira, you can thank Greta for fixing you a nice hot bath." Tobby and I stood there in the hall waiting breathlessly, with great expectation. I'm not sure what I expected—an apology? a smile? a hug? a thank you?

There was a long moment of awkward silence, and then he turned to me and looked me square in the eye and in a low grumble said, "I run my own bath water," and promptly yanked out the stopper and slammed the door. Tobby and I stood there (as Aunt Sky would say, "lookin' foolish out the face)." We were speechless for what seemed like a long time. Finally, one of us bust out laughing; I don't remember who. We went back to Tobby's room and mocked Uncle Ira saying the words, "I run my own bath water," over and over again. We laughed and snickered so long, 'til Aunt Tee finally scolded us both and made us go to bed.

Uncle Bud

JET BLACK

To everything there is a season,
and a time to every purpose under the heaven:
A time to love, a time to hate;
a time of war, and a time of peace;
a time to weep, and a time to laugh;
a time to mourn, and a time to dance.

ECCLESIASTES 3: 1, 8, 4

The days came and went, and the evenings slipped into the next day, and Mama received a letter from her long lost brother Bud.

Dearest Emma,

I will leave Arkansas by train on August 27th. Need a place to lay my head. My plan is to arrive in Chicago on Labor Day. Many thanks to you and Clem for your help in this matter.

Sincerely,
Your Brother, Bud

Uncle Bud was Mama's baby brother. He was born Q.W. Whitlock but had been called Bud all his life because he had always been small in stature. It always tickled me that Q and W were not the initials of his first and middle names. Q.W. was his name.

He was a Viet Nam War veteran who we had heard about only in whispered conversations. Aunt Sky said that he'd gone mad after the war and should be institutionalized, that he was a wayward gypsy forced to move from pillar to post because he practiced voodoo. She said, "Never look directly in his eyes. They're like black pools that'll hypnotize you. And his fingertips are burnt, everyone of 'em; probably from them satanic rituals." Aunt Tee said he wasn't crazy at all, just shell-shocked and a little eccentric. There had been talk of him often cleaning a gun he kept in a mysterious cigar box decorated with old coins, along with rumors of womanizing and wife beating. Aunt Sky also said he had killed a man once.

When Labor Day came, it was a huge celebration. It was one of the hottest days of the year. Daddy and Chappy Smith were in the backyard under the shade of the big oak tree grilling ribs, burgers, hot dogs, and corn on the cob, offering up delicious talk about the Senior Bishop's new, young wife. Mama, Aunt Tee, and Aunt Sky were in the kitchen preparing side dishes and, as usual, serving up their own little tidbits of gossip. All the kids were sent outside. Daddy had cut up slices of chilled watermelon to cool us off when we took breaks from playing in the hot sun. The heat had drawn people out on their porches with their kitchen chairs, their card tables, and their televisions. It was so hot, someone had opened the corner fire hydrant and tied a two-by-four to it so the water sprayed up and out like a giant waterfall. Every kid within a six-block radius came to dart in and out of the refreshing, illegal water feature.

Shane and I were sitting on the porch drying off when the cab pulled up. He was finally here. This mysterious man, the enigma we had never seen but had heard about all our lives, was about to emerge from the back seat of a black livery cab. It was hard to look directly at the cab because there was a glare from the sun that hurt my eyes. Everything I had ever heard about Uncle Bud quickly flashed through my mind as I sat transfixed in the moment.

I couldn't move. Then the car door opened, and he tossed out a small piece of luggage and a large green army bag knotted at the top. One polished, brown, lace-up Stacy Adams stepped out, then the other. He wore brown slacks that were pleated and cuffed. And though his white shirt was rumpled, I could tell it had been laundered and starched. And as he stood there taking one last draw from his cigarette, he reminded me of an old black and white photograph from the 1930s. He was striking. He stood about five feet five inches tall. His skin was a smooth mix of red and caramel. His jet black, wavy hair was slicked back and glistened in the sun. I desperately wanted to see his eyes, but he wore dark sunglasses as he walked towards us going into the house. And as he did, Shane and I parted like the Red Sea to let him pass. We scurried in behind him, and Mama quickly shooed us back outside. She said they had to talk grown folks business. We hurried to an open screened window to listen. They spoke in hushed voices for a time and then broke out in thunderous laughter. Shortly after that, Aunt Mae and Aunt Sadie also arrived to welcome their long lost brother.

Mama showed Uncle Bud where he could settle in and wash up, while Daddy and Chappy Smith brought in succulent pieces of meat from the grill. Aunt Tee and Aunt Sky organized the food on the sideboard—all the meats together, then vegetables, then starches, then breads, then desserts. Later, when we all sat down to eat, Daddy let Uncle Bud sit at the head of the table. He was still wearing his sunglasses. He was flanked on either side by Mama and Aunt Tee. Daddy sat at the opposite end, and the other grown-ups filled in. Two folding tables had been set up for all the children.

It was a huge feast and a dual celebration—the end of summer and the beginning of Uncle Bud's life with us. After Daddy said grace, he gave special thanks that Uncle Bud was now a part of our family. It felt like Thanksgiving with all the chatter around the table, the passing of rolls and potato salad, ribs and black-eyed peas. And as I partook in the festivities, I cautiously watched Uncle Bud. He had a huge appetite, but took his time, chewing ever so slowly, like he was savoring every morsel of food. But amidst all the rant and prattle, Uncle Bud never uttered a word. Then Daddy raised his glass and said, "To Bud. May your time here be the best of your years." Uncle Bud then took off his glasses and said simply, "Thank you." I saw them, his eyes, for the very first time. And when he looked at me, his eyes penetrated mine. He locked me into his gaze, and I couldn't look away. They were absolutely jet black, dark pools that held joy and pain, wisdom and secrets—but the kindest eyes I had ever seen. After a moment Uncle Bud too raised his glass, and everyone else followed suit.

Over the next several weeks, he was secretly under surveillance. There was no extra bedroom for him, only an open space on the second floor that Daddy filled with donated furniture and partitioned off with two massive, portable room dividers. We kids cautiously took turns peeking through the openings to see what he was doing. He was our Boo Radley. This dark, mysterious character was now living among us. We loved the secrecy, the snooping. It excited us. It gave us purpose. Peeking through the cracks, we could see glimpses of Uncle Bud's life neatly placed about his dresser: a picture of a beautiful woman with sandy-colored eyes, a couple of army medals, the infamous cigar box with its shiny exterior, four little cloth dolls no bigger than your hand propped up against the mirror, and another picture of two small children with his same kind eyes.

The whole month of September rolled by, and he had done nothing out of the ordinary. He made frequent trips to the refrigerator, the bathroom, and out back to smoke cigarettes. But on October 1st, Uncle Bud did something we had never seen him do before. He left the house. He was gone about two hours. When he returned, he had two bags of groceries. All the perishable items were put in the refrigerator and labeled, "BUD DO NOT TOUCH." The non-perishables were taken to his room along with three small brown paper bags. About two hours later, a man we had never met before emerged from Uncle Bud's room. He was lively and loud and most entertaining.

The days turned into months, and months turned into years. Where Aunt Sky had turned over a sober new leaf, most of the time Uncle Bud was drunk as a skunk. So Thanksgiving and Christmas became interesting holidays in our house. It wasn't Thanksgiving without Mama's potato salad, sweet potato pie, and her famous duck and dressing. Aunt Sky's specialty was chittlins, which had to be surgically cleaned before eating. There were so many, the only place large enough to clean them was the bathtub. And they smelled abominable. She put white potatoes in the pots while they were cooking; that always helped with the odor. But when they were done, oh, they were delectable, wrinkled delicacies. When Uncle Bud wasn't under the influence, his specialty was coon. Yes, raccoon. I'm still not sure if he killed the coon himself or if he purchased it from a specialty meat shop. But the skinned, roasted varmint was downright scary. Every year, when we'd open the roaster, that coon would be staring at you with its eyes wide open, teeth in a scowl, and claws poised for combat, like he was fighting for his life until the very end. I could never bring myself to partake of the coon, but Mama said it was delicious.

The Christmas tree was put up the day before Thanksgiving. Mama preferred an artificial tree. She also liked it decorated within an inch of its life: candy canes, ribbon, tinsel, popcorn streamers, lights, and beautiful ornaments. We were all in a festive mood and decorating the tree on Thanksgiving eve when the call came. Aunt Mae had died. She had been found in the stairwell of her workplace, still in her coat and hat, her hand still clutching her purse. It was a hard Thanksgiving that year. Trying to have thankful hearts with a loss like that is easier said than done.

The news of her passing rippled through the family, and the infighting began. There were so many children with so many differing opinions. They fought about where the service should be held, what songs should be sung, who should give the eulogy, and who should be excluded from the obituary. After much deliberation, her service was held at her church and she was eulogized by her pastor. In the end, it was about celebrating the life of a woman beloved by her family and cherished by those whose lives were blessed by the work she did. The church was overflowing, and people were waiting outside in hopes of getting in to say goodbye. Hundreds of people had come to pay tribute to a woman they dearly loved, whose life had touched theirs through something so simple—a hot meal. But for Aunt Mae, a hot meal was much more than that. It was sustenance, it was relationship, it was community, and it was love.

Uncle Bud didn't drink that day. He had written a poem in honor of Aunt Mae. And he delivered it with a clear head and a heavy heart.

> Dear Sister,
> I don't know why death gathers those we love so much.
> Maybe there is special work to be done in heaven
> That can only be done by the strong of spirit.
> Today and always I'll hear the sound of your voice,
> In the trees,
> In the wind,
> In the thunder,
> In the rolling waves.
> You will always hold a hallowed place in my heart.

His words washed over me like water in a stream, and I couldn't help reflecting back over Aunt Mae's life and contemplating the unexpected trajectory. And I smiled at the thought of this woman, who in the wake of the dreadful vicissitudes of life, had come back roaring like a lion.

We were all still reeling from Aunt Mae's passing when we lost Aunt Sadie. She went into the hospital on a Monday with a bad case of pneumonia and never came out.

Three weeks later, we were laying her to rest. I remember standing over her casket and seeing her for the last time. She looked simply beautiful lying there, with that velvety skin, just like she was asleep. Aunt Tee fixed her hair just the way she liked it, swept up in a neat bun. She looked so radiant, like she wasn't gone at all. Gilbert Earl was there with his wife and children. He seemed to take it awful hard. CeCe was shrouded in black from head to toe. Aunt Sky said she looked like a black widow spider. And Big Otha attended the service. He embraced Gilbert Earl and his grandchildren, but the two of them never acknowledged CeCe, not one word. They hadn't spoken in years, and that day was no different. But CeCe didn't seem to mind. She seemed to take it all in stride. She was very elegant that day, regal even. She greeted family and friends from the front pew like a queen holding court. CeCe had made all the funeral arrangements and made sure every flower that arrived was white to match the color of Aunt Sadie's dress. Every detail was lovely and, as funerals go, flawlessly executed— exactly as Aunt Sadie would have wanted it.

At the burial ground, CeCe was the last to leave. She said she had to see her mother one last time. And she wouldn't leave until the undertaker granted her this final request. When they opened the casket, CeCe didn't weep or show visible signs of grief. There was no lamentation. But she slowly lifted the thin veil that had cloaked her face. She then gracefully leaned down and kissed her mother on the cheek and said, "Thank you." Mama said it was only a week later she learned that Aunt Sadie had left the two rental properties solely to CeCe.

CHAPTER ELEVEN

Sunday Mornin' Bliss

& SATURDAY NIGHT BLUES

It was shortly after the passing of Aunt Mae and Aunt Sadie that Aunt Sky's granddaughter, Tina, came to live with us. She was a pretty, round-faced, caramel-skinned child, with the longest legs I'd ever seen on a girl.

And Tina joined the choir. She had been blessed with a few gifts and graces, but singing wasn't one of them. Her voice was loud and shrill, and the girl couldn't carry a tune if you put it in a bucket. Despite that, Aunt Sky wrote a song for Tina and requested that we sing it at an upcoming church event. It was a dreadful song she proudly entitled, "Oh Lawd, oh Lawdy." We hated that song, but we loved Aunt Sky. During rehearsals we could barely get through the chorus without breaking out in laughter. But we were determined to support Aunt Sky. We were at our annual church convention, and the master of ceremonies called us up to render an A selection.

We took our positions on the podium, and Tobby began to play the oh so dreaded song. Aunt Sky rose from her seat beaming with pride as Tina approached the microphone. She was visibly nervous and missed her cue to begin the song. So Tobby played the intro again. We all took a deep breath as Aunt Sky shouted encouragement from the audience to reassure her, "That's alright, Baby! Take your time!" Tobby gave her the cue again, and this time she didn't miss it. "Amazing grace how sweeeeeeet the sooooound. . . ." The girl hit notes we had never heard before, notes so piercing and flat you literally wanted to plug your ears.

A snicker escaped from Hazel's lips, and that was the beginning of the end. The debut of Aunt Sky's new song had taken flight and was crashing and burning before our eyes. The laughter caught on like wildfire. When it was time for the choir to come in, we were deep in the throes of laughter. It wasn't loud, hysterical laughter, but rather the uncontrollable, embarrassed laughter—the heads bowed, eyes closed, shoulders shaking, and tears streaming down your face, completely silent kind of laughter. Tobby was doubled over on the organ, but still managed to play the choir intro four more times. And each time he played it the funnier it got. We stood in front of that packed church and never sang a note. After the fourth attempt, Tobby ended the song, and we walked shamefacedly back to our seats and kept our heads down for the remainder of the service.

On the way home in the van, Aunt Sky was silent. Mama and Daddy said nothing. And we were too embarrassed to even utter a word. The next Sunday after church, Aunt Tee and Tobby came to the house for dinner. Aunt Sky and Tina came upstairs and joined us. We ate dinner politely and made quiet small talk while Mama served dessert. A car horn blew out front. It was Tina's godmother. Aunt Sky kissed her and watched her as she bounded out the front door.

Just as the door closed behind her, Aunt Sky turned to us and said, "How come nobody told me that child can't sing?" Not one of us knew how to respond. The last thing any of us wanted to do was hurt Aunt Sky's feelings. "That girl hit notes last Sunday that made me want to plug my ears. Until last Sunday, I didn't know how bad it was!" Then she threw her head back and enveloped us with that life-giving laugh. It only took a few moments for her words to settle in the air, and then laughter erupted around the table. Aunt Sky made Tobby promise to give Tina singing lessons, and Tobby made Aunt Sky promise not to write any more songs.

Months went by, and church life was run of the mill. Daddy

preached messages heaving with fire and brimstone. Aunt Tee hosted a number of events (the Annual Women's Tea, the Annual Women's Luncheon, and the Annual Church Bazaar) to raise money for the building fund. And Aunt Sky was always our Sunday morning bliss. She forever had a burning testimony to share with the congregation, followed by a song, which to this day, I think she would make up on the spot. This Sunday, the temperature was just shy of 100 degrees. After testifying about how God had turned her life around from being a raging alcoholic to becoming a raving disciple of Jesus, she said, "Saints, I am on fire for the Lord"! And then she broke into song:

> Just like fire
> Shut up in my bones
> Just like fire
> Shut up in my bones
> Holy Ghost fire
> Shut up in my bones
> Holy Ghost fire
> Shut up in my bones

It was blistering. The air conditioning had gone out, and fans were being used to cool the sanctuary. As I fanned myself profusely, I thought, "Why did she have to sing that song hot as it is?"

People were starting to leave because of the heat. As the service drew to a close, the visiting pastor made an altar call for those with a desire to join the church and those standing in the need of prayer. As the choir began to sing, "Come to Jesus, Come to Jesus, Come to Jesus just now," a youngish woman approached the altar. She wore a flowing yellow dress with a matching hat. As the pastor met her there, she whispered her prayer concern in his ear. He then beckoned for the elders who made a circle around her. Mama and Aunt Sky joined them at the altar, and the pastor began to pray:

> Dear Heavenly Father, there is one who has come and is
> standin' in the need of prayer. Lord, we come against the
> spirit of promiscuity. We plead the blood over her life,

and ask that Jesus would stand at every gate: her ear gate so that she may be careful what she allows herself to hear, her mouth gate so that her conversation will be chaste, her eye gate so that she is mindful what she allows her eyes to see. And lastly Lord, her vagina gate.

Just as he said that, Aunt Sky opened one eye to peek at Mama, who was standing next to her, and their shoulders began to shake. It is a blur what the minister said after that. There were shoulders shaking all over the church.

Down through the years, at every family gathering, somebody would say, "Aunt Sky, tell us about the altar call for the woman in the yellow dress." That story was always just as funny as the first time she told it. Whenever Aunt Sky would recall the tale, she'd laugh hysterically saying, "Baeeeby, when that man said 'vagina gate' I like to peed in my pants." Aunt Sky's stories never got old, and we never tired of hearing them. They were delicious recounts from her memory that spanned decades. They were snatches of history told in a way that always left us wanting more. She was a deep well that never ran dry.

I spent a lot of time at Aunt Sky's. We enjoyed each other's company. Many nights we'd just sit at her kitchen table. She loved sharing her stories, and I loved hearing them. Skylene Fae Whitlock had lived an interesting life. She made her living cleaning the homes of two white families. She never complained, because she said the O'Brians and the Sutherlins treated her like family and gave generous bonuses around the holidays. Aunt Sky always had a story to tell.

And the long scar she wore on the right side of her face told a story all its own. Before she met Uncle Gus, she had many lovers and craved the nightlife and all that went with it. She knew the inside of many a Chicago nightclub and bar, and most of the bartenders knew her by name. "What'll it be tonight, Sky?" they'd ask with enthusiasm and familiarity as she'd blaze into a club. She had been a good-looking, henna-colored woman with a curvaceous body who had a wild and insatiable hunger for life and laughter. She was saucy and vivacious with a sharp tongue, but an equally sharp mind. She could easily hold a man's attention with just her conversation. And she knew how to woo him in other ways if she so desired.

It was one of those nights at her kitchen table when Aunt Sky told me the story of how she got the long scar on her face. She began, "I was feelin' gooood that night. I had just left your Aunt Tee's chair. And my hair was fried, dyed, and laid to the side!" Then she did that thing I loved to see her do. She threw her head back, and laughed that deep, lusty laugh.

"Your Aunt Tee had just given me a mess o' fresh curls that were bouncin' around my shoulders, and I had to go out that night! You know how it is when you've got that fresh-out-the-beauty-shop hair. You want to show it off! 'Cause once you sleep on it, you can never duplicate that hairdo. So I went home and bathed, and painted my nails red, and put on a little red dress that hit me in all the right places. Oh, I was hot-to-trot! I stepped off up in Rick's Club that night like I owned the place. Rick's was one of the many night spots I would frequent. Rick and I were sweet on each other, and I knew he would be there 'cause he always worked on Saturday nights.

"He saw me as soon as I walked in because the regulars were there and announced my arrival. 'My girl Sky, umph, umph, umph. You look good enough to eat! . . . Sky, Sky, Sky! Ooh-wee! Girl, you wearin' that red dress!' Rick was surrounded by a group of women gathered like spring hens around a young cock. He broke free, cleared a space for me at the bar, and gestured for me to have a seat. As I sauntered towards him, the walk was slow, deliberate, and easy. I swayed my hips in a way that made him stir in his pants. I could feel his eyes all over me. The lusty heat between us was so thick it was suffocating. His fingertips felt hot as they touched the small of my back, and his hand guided me onto the seat. He poured me a vodka tonic, and I planned to nurse it all night, 'cause I wanted to look good all night. Baby, always remember, if you drink more than one, it shows on your face. And you ain't nearly as cute when you walk out as when you walked in. Believe me I know.

"I had gotten up to go to the ladies room. The music was loud, and the dance floor was filled with glistening bodies gyrating and shimmying to a B.B. King tune. When I returned, there was a young woman sitting in my seat. She was wearing a black, strapless dress with her hair slicked back. I politely tapped her on her shoulder and asked her to move. I told her that I had only left momentarily to powder my nose. In a slow, monotone voice she said, 'This my seat, everybody knows that. You betta ask somebody.' She lazily rolled her eyes and took her time slowly turning her back to me. I could feel my anger gathering force, and the blood begin to drain from my face, and my fingertips started to tingle. Before I realized it, I had spun her around on that bar stool so she faced me. In the split second it took her to get around, she'd smashed a glass and, with its jagged edge, split my face wide open from temple to jawbone. The next day, I woke up in the hospital with forty-eight stitches holding the right side of my face together.

"Yeah, I had a hot head and too much mouth, and I got the battle scars to prove it. I later found out . . . she was Rick's wife." That was the only time Aunt Sky revealed a part of her life to me that wasn't wrapped in her signature humor.

CHAPTER TWELVE

Shell-Shocked

1967

On the first of every month, the ritual was always the same. Uncle Bud would cash his disability check, get his groceries and his liquor, and leave two crisp one hundred dollar bills on the kitchen table for rent. And he was drunk for the next two weeks or until his liquor ran out.

With the drink in him, Uncle Bud was a joy to be around. He was a great storyteller, gregarious and animated. He'd tell us terrifying tales from Viet Nam about bombs exploding in the barracks or friends being killed alongside him in the trenches. He talked of a torrid affair with a woman while he was married to his wife. The mistress was a beautiful woman with long brown hair and eyes the color of sand. And he was deathly afraid of a group of people called Geechees. When sharing their legacy and practices, he always spoke in hushed tones and constantly checked over his shoulder to ensure that no Geechee was in earshot. He said they were very tiny people who practiced witchcraft and voodoo and would kill you on the spot if you crossed them. As time went on, we knew when Uncle Bud was drunk before he entered a room. His footsteps always gave him away. He walked hard, as if bricks were tied to his feet.

Uncle Bud was very private and always kept his partitions closed. One evening I came upstairs, and one of the partitions was ajar. Other than the sound of light snoring, it was very quiet. I tiptoed over to the opening and peered in. Uncle Bud lay there asleep, and someone was sleeping next to him. I wondered if this was the beautiful mistress in the photograph. As I eased in to get a closer look, I could see this was a different woman. She wasn't pretty at all. Her features were hard and chiseled. Her hair was short and nappy like a man's. Oh my God! It was a man! As I watched in stunned silence, something bitter rose in my throat, and I remember feeling tiny little prickles on the back of my neck and under my arms. I stood there for the longest time staring at the lover and thinking to myself, "God, he sure is ug-g-gly." A rustling from downstairs broke my trance-like state. As I slowly began backing out of the room to leave, the lover shifted, and a perfectly round breast was exposed. A scarcely audible gasp escaped my lips. I was relieved. A weight was lifted. She was ugly, but by God, she was a woman. I smiled to myself as I eased out of the room and quietly closed the partition.

When Uncle Bud wasn't in an altered state, he was quiet and unassuming. And he was very meticulous about certain things. He'd sit and polish his shoes until they shone like new. He'd wash, starch, and press his own shirts. He kept his little partitioned corner of the house neat and tidy. And I learned that his fingertips were stained brown, not from satanic rituals, but from tobacco, because he rolled his own cigarettes.

Uncle Bud never claimed to be a Christian. But he had a strong belief in higher powers. He respected the sovereignty of God, but he also believed in the power of voodoo. Sometimes when I'd peek through the cracks of the partitions, the little dolls would be carefully arranged on his dresser in strange positions. Sometimes they'd be bound or pierced clean through with sharp objects. Once, when Uncle Bud was out on his first-of-the-month pilgrimage to buy groceries and liquor, I opened the partition and slipped into his little sanctuary to closely inspect the peculiar shrine he fashioned so neatly on his dresser. I lightly ran my fingers across each tiny doll, his army medals, each picture, and the shiny cigar box. It was exquisite, extremely smooth to the touch, and every coin sparkled like new. And then I noticed that the lock was open. A gasp escaped my lips, and I swallowed hard twice before opening the burnished box. I had never seen a gun up close before. I could feel my heart leaping against my chest, and my hands were shaking as I removed the lock and lifted the lid. And as the room's light illuminated the contents of the box, I was completely overcome by what I saw. It was the woman with the sandy colored eyes. The picture was haunting. And the obituary read:

Addie Samuels
Born into life May 11, 1936
Born into eternity November 17, 1967

And as I pulled it out to read on, tiny mementos fell from between the folds of the paper: a ring embedded with one red ruby, a lock of hair held together by a small, bejeweled hairpin, and a newspaper clipping. She had been killed in a horrible car crash in the fall of 1967. Tears swelled in my eyes as I completely understood why he treasured this small box. He hadn't been cleaning a gun at all, but lovingly shining the coins that adorned this sacred chest he'd made to house the memories of his lost love. As I carefully replaced the items, I felt as though I'd found the last piece of his life's puzzle and was setting it firmly in place. I felt like I now truly knew the man so few people understood. Aunt Tee had been right all along. He was eccentric and maybe a little shell-shocked, but he certainly wasn't crazy. He was just a man who had experienced more than his share of tragedy and loss, and was just trying in his own authentic way to cope with it all.

Spring came and brought with it a warm wind of thirsty expectation. All the girls were getting ready for junior prom. Daddy was totally against it because he knew there would surely be boys, dancing, drinking, and God knows what else. Mama persuaded him very strategically and lovingly over a two-week period, assuring him that I could be trusted to be the fastidious young lady they had brought me up to be. Mama was so wise; it was like a dance with him. Instinctively she knew when to hold on tight and when to let go, when to push and when to pull away, when to lead and when to follow.

Under some protest and against his better judgment, he acquiesced. I squealed with joy when Mama told me. She had somehow managed to sooth the savage beast in him. Having gotten over that hurdle, I had yet another one to conquer. I didn't have a date. Every other girl I knew was going and had her dress already. Sylvia was wearing a fabulous red dress, and Yolanda was wearing purple. I was happy for them, but I was discouraged and a little envious. It was three weeks till prom and not a prospect in sight when Stephan Thomas came a knocking. He wasn't real popular, because he wasn't an athlete, but he was on the debate team for Harper High School, so I felt he'd be a good date. Yes, he'd do just fine. So, I started shopping for the perfect dress. I tried on dress after dress after dress. They were too short or too long, too big or too tight, too this or too that. And then I tried on a dress that made me feel like Cinderella on her way to the ball. It was powder blue, with an empire waist, spaghetti straps, and folds and folds of billowing chiffon that stopped just above the knee. I tried on a pair of strappy, black, patent leather sandals. Flawless.

Aunt Tee insisted on doing my hair for the special occasion. She said I had graduated from the usual press and curl, that this affair warranted a relaxer and a spanking new cut. I arrived at Aunt Tee's that morning and settled contentedly into her chair. She put a plastic cape around my neck and slathered something that looked like petroleum jelly around my edges, then she applied the relaxer. It went on cool at first, and then after several minutes the lye started to burn. She led me over to the sink and vigorously shampooed my hair. After conditioning and blowing it dry, it was bone straight, and she cut it into a blunt little bob. It was shiny and bouncy, and the slightest head-turn made my hair go "swish."

I left Aunt Tee's and stopped in Nail City to get a manicure and pedicure. I wanted to sparkle from head to toe. The festivities started at 7:00 p.m. Stephan was picking me up at 6:30, so I started getting ready about 4:30. I enjoyed a warm bath and masked my face. I remembered CeCe's make up tutorial: a light layer of foundation with a dusting of blush. I drew perfect brows and luscious ruby lips. I slipped on my blue chiffon dress and zipped it on the side. It was so elegant with my new hair cut. I couldn't wait for Stephan to see me. I slid on the sexy shoes and walked into the living room where Mama 'n Nem were waiting. They clapped and cheered as I made my princess-like entrance. Mama and Aunt Sky gushed endlessly over the dress, while Ray and Shane took pictures. Uncle Bud came through and whistled flirtingly at me. Clem Jr. kissed me on the cheek and said, "Dang, you clean up good!" Daddy gave me a quick wink before leaving and reiterating what time Prince Charming needed to have Cinderella back home before the carriage turned into a pumpkin.

It was a beautiful May evening, so, I stepped out onto the front porch to await Stephan's arrival. I breathed in the warm air and gazed up at the heavens, a million stars twinkling back at me. It was 6:30. "He'll be here any minute," I whispered to myself. Mama came out to give me a handkerchief in case I needed it. She told me again how pretty I looked and fussed with my hair a bit, then went back inside. I looked at my watch. It was 6:40. Stephan was apparently running late. I dashed inside to call his house, but no one answered. He was evidently on his way. I stopped in the bathroom to do a final check of my hair and makeup. "I love it," I said to myself as I turned out the light and headed back to the porch. "Nobody answered the phone when I called his house, so, he's obviously on his way," I announced to Mama and Aunt Sky who were anxiously waiting in the living room.

Clem Jr., Ray, and Shane gave me their brotherly words of acumen as they all left the house: "Hey, don't do nothin' I wouldn't do. . . . He betta git you back here in one piece. . . . He betta have you back on time. You know what happens when the clock strikes midnight!" We all laughed as I followed them out to the car and watched them drive away.

It was now 7:00. I'm not certain, but it was probably fear that began to churn ever so faintly in the pit of my stomach. I turned to look up at the house. Mama and Aunt Sky were standing in the picture window, smiles of expectation still in the corners of their mouths. I returned to the porch and paced back and forth.

I paced for two hours. At 9:00 Mama finally came out and asked, "Are you hungry?" I nodded yes. "Well, I got some chicken and dumplings." I smiled. She knew it was my favorite. "Let me help you out of that dress."

"No," I said. "I wanna keep it on a while."

She nodded in agreement. She made three place settings—for me, herself, and Aunt Sky. As Mama filled our plates, Aunt Sky began her declarations, "Honey, it's his loss. Shoot, he don't know what he's missin'. You was gone be the prettiest thing at the prom! I bet he wasn't cute no way."

I loved me some Aunt Sky. She knew just what to say to lighten the mood. They sat with me at the kitchen table for a long time. Mama's chicken and dumplings were surely comfort food that night, and their healing words were like the balm in Gilead bathing my wounded spirit. Uncle Bud came through the kitchen to smoke a cigarette out back. I kissed Mama and Aunt Sky and thanked them for setting my teenage world back on its axle.

I walked out the kitchen's squeaky screen door and sat next to Uncle Bud on the top step. For the longest time neither one of us uttered a word. I was content just watching the smoke from his cigarette snake into the night air.

"So, he stood you up, huh?" He finally asked between puffs.

"Yeah." I replied, not feeling the sting of it anymore, thanks to Mama and Aunt Sky.

"Can you keep a secret?" he asked. I nodded yes. He pulled out a silver flask and two tiny shot glasses. He filled them to the rim, and on the count of three we downed the miniature shots of bourbon.

It initially burned the back of my throat and then was nothing but warm and smooth on the way down.

"Don't take it too hard. You just gettin' started. You'll come to learn we men are strange animals. We're hard to live with, but you'll find that you don't ever want to live without us."

Sleep came easy that night. I'm not sure if it was the hours of angst or the bourbon.

CHAPTER THIRTEEN

What List?

THE MEASURE OF A MAN

Daddy was a strong disciplinarian. "Spare the rod, spoil the child" was biblical, but it was also his mantra. Before a whipping he'd talk to you. The opening dialogue was always calm and conversational, like a therapy session. He'd give you a chance to tell your side of the story and or apologize. And just when you thought he might let you off the hook, he'd wear you out with his belt. That was one thing that always seemed to go in slow motion, the sight of Daddy taking off his belt just before a whipping.

I got my last whipping when I turned seventeen. Coming directly home from school was not an option, it was mandatory. This particular day I ignored the cardinal rule and attended a basketball game with Yolanda. Daddy had always spoken against basketball games. I guess boys chasing a ball and aiming it at a hoop was also somehow Satan-related. At any rate, we were not allowed to take pleasure in such carnal indulgences.

When I got home three hours late, Daddy wasn't there. I was in the clear, or so I thought. Mama told me he had indeed been home but was out running errands. I went to my room and stayed there, thinking maybe I'd be asleep by the time he got home. I was asleep, but was awakened by a slap, his rough hand across my face. "Where were you?!" Another slap. "I said, where were you?!" I was dazed and disoriented, but I had to think fast. I knew telling the truth would warrant a full-scale whipping. So I lied.

"Me and Yolanda were just out walkin'."

"Walkin' where?" he asked.

"Walkin' on 79th Street," my voice shaking in dishonesty.

Daddy replied, "Oh, so you a street walker now?!" And he commenced to thrashing me across my arms and legs with a short razor strap. I didn't deserve this. I felt numb, and I refused to cry. I counted each stinging lash as it made puffy, red marks across my tender flesh: one . . . two . . . three . . . four . . . five . . . six . . . seven . . . eight . . . nine lashes.

He raised his arm for the tenth time, and Mama cried out imploringly, "Clem! She's on her period!" And then in almost a whisper she said, "And she's got to have children someday."

I'll never forget the look on his face. He was completely stricken, with his hand mid-air. A few seconds later he lowered his arm, and the offending object dropped at his feet, and he left the room a different man.

And Mama, sweet Mama, bathed my wounds in witch hazel and mineral oil that night. She was always there to calm, soothe, and offer words of wisdom and healing. Difficult times like these were always met with tenderness and grace.

That last whipping was a defining moment in both of our lives, Daddy and me. I was standing at the threshold of womanhood. And I realized that day that in my sixteen years I had never done anything bad enough to warrant the whippings I'd endured. And the look on his face said that he regretted how hard he had been on me, not just that day, but throughout my life. And although he never said, "I'm sorry," his eyes spoke the words I knew his lips couldn't utter. From that day forward, Daddy never raised a hand to me. When disciplinary action was needed, he only raised his voice.

I got accepted to several universities but settled on Rust College, a small Methodist college in Holly Springs, Mississippi. Mama was happy, proud, and sad all at the same time, because not only was

I leaving home, Uncle Bud was leaving too. His daughter Sherri bought a house in Las Vegas and offered him a room with a view and his own private bath. It was bittersweet as he packed his spare belongings and folded back the partitions for the first time in many years.

Laughter and tears flowed as we said our goodbyes at Chicago's O'Hare Airport. I hugged him tightly and told him to call often. Then he slipped a small, black velvet bag into my hand. "This will bring you good luck and ward off evil spirits." And as he turned to wave a final farewell, he again reminded me of an old black and white photograph, with his cuffed wool pants, starched white shirt, shiny black shoes, and that old green army bag thrown over his shoulder. As he walked out of sight, I opened the velvet sack to find a polished coin he had removed from his hallowed box.

The day I left for college is a moment in time that will be forever burned into my memory and my heart. Mama hated saying goodbye in public. So she kissed me and held me tight and shared some final words of wisdom before I left for the bus station. The ride to the station was awkward and silent. There were so many things I wanted to say to Daddy that I couldn't even begin to articulate. And I sensed that he had a floodgate of things he wanted to share with me, but somehow couldn't form the words.

Finally, we arrived at the bus station, and Daddy turned off the engine. After a long pause he said, "Remember who you are and everything your Mother and I have taught you, and you'll do just fine. And if you ever need anything, we're just a phone call away." And with that, he quickly opened his door and began unloading my luggage from the car.

Daddy followed me onto the bus with my carry-on bag and stowed it over my seat. And before I sat down, he reached for my hand and kissed my left cheek. He held that kiss for what seemed like an eternity. It was only about twenty seconds, but those timeless few moments encompassed my whole life to that point with my father. Water leaped into my eyes and an awful pain rose in my throat as I fought back the tears. Daddy was true to form that day. He didn't say "I love you." In fact, the word love was never uttered, even at this important juncture in my life. And at that moment I had the most amazing epiphany. I realized at that instant that the unspoken word had never been voiced but had always been demonstrated. He had been our guardian, our protector, and he had loved us the only way he knew how and to the best of his ability. He was just a country boy with a seventh grade education, with limited memories of his own father. That day I knew unequivocally that Mama and we five kids were clearly the most important people in his life.

Ohhh . . . so many memories ran through my mind: How he'd never been unfaithful to Mama or abusive to her in any way. Daddy never smoked or drank liquor. And he never once used a curse word in our presence. Many times it was Daddy who had hot food waiting for us when we came home from school for lunch. It was Daddy who pushed us for hours on the swings in the park. It was Daddy who packed shoeboxes full of snacks, sandwiches, and fried chicken on road trips down south. And it was Daddy who instilled in us a work ethic, moral values, social responsibility, and self esteem. That was love.

There is simply nothing like the Black college experience. There is a certain bond, a camaraderie, and a kinship that rests on a Black college campus. The minute I stepped off that Greyhound bus, I knew I had arrived at my home away from home—a small campus with green, well-manicured grounds and magnolia trees in full bloom. Rust College was buzzing with in-coming freshman, upperclassmen, fraternities, sororities, and international students. I settled into the freshman dormitory, and Mama had made sure it would be well appointed with the things I needed for my first semester.

I got my class schedule and settled into college life. The first two weeks were a whirlwind of activities: a basketball game between Rust and Old Miss, a step show that featured sororities and fraternities in full regalia, a choir concert, a chess tournament, a fashion show, a one-act play, and at least a dozen parties. My head was spinning, but I loved it. I was there to get an education, but I was determined to show up at all events and attend every party—that was an education in itself.

So I began to prioritize. I studied early in the morning so I could grace events and parties well into the night, and I would sleep between classes. That worked out famously. I immediately started dating a young man named Thomas Canada. He was tall and fair-skinned, with hazel eyes and a devilish grin. There was Bad Boy running through his veins, but that intrigued me. We ended up at all the parties.

I had just come in from an all-nighter. I was wearily removing my makeup when the phone rang. I answered, thinking it was Thomas, but it was Mama's voice on the other end. "Hey, honey. I hate to call you with this news . . . but your Uncle Bud passed last night."

My heart sank, and the tears had already started to saturate my eyes. "What happened?" I asked softly.

"He died gently in his sleep. Sherri said he just up and died, peaceful-like and quiet."

A fresh void hovered in my heart for the whole week, until Mama called and narrated the details of his honorable, military home going. It was a crisp fall day. And she said it was just like in the movies, with a single soldier trumpeting Taps and that stunning gun salute, most fitting for a Viet Nam war veteran, and a lasting tribute to our precious Uncle Bud.

There was always something happening on campus. And I was right in the thick of things. I was asked to sing in an upcoming talent show for Delta Sigma Theta. I was in the auditorium rehearsing the number when a young man walked in and sat in the front row. He was average height, about five feet nine inches tall, and very stylishly dressed. When I finished the song, his singular applause ricocheted vociferously off the walls of the empty theater. As he began mounting the stairs to join me on stage, I thought, "Wow, he's gorgeous." His features were silky and black; his skin, his mustache, his eyebrows, and his lashes were so dark and long, I could swear I felt a breeze when he batted his eyes.

"You have a beautiful voice," he said. "You should join the A cappella Choir. We're holding auditions tomorrow—this building, Room 201, 4:30. Hope you can make it."

He gathered his things and just before he exited he said, "By the way, my name is Dennis Oglesby."

I was all set to join the Gospel Choir, but the invitation peaked my interest. I showed up. I sang an old church hymn and found out that day that I was one of three new members. The choir met five days a week. Not only did they sing gospels, but anthems and spirituals which broadened my vocal range and music vocabulary. Dennis was one of the star soloists in the choir and took full credit for recruiting me.

He also took the liberty of asking me out. I was dating Thomas, so I turned him down. On top of that, he wasn't my type. I had a list of things I wanted in a boyfriend:

The List
1. Christian
2. Six feet tall
3. Bow-legged
4. An athlete
5. Fair complexion

Dennis was none of the things on my list. But he was persistent. Rust College didn't prescribe to coed dormitories. So anytime a male came to visit, it was announced over the women's dorm intercom. I was just getting out of the shower when I heard, "Greta Lacy, you have a guest in the lobby. Greta Lacy, you have a guest in the lobby." I quickly threw on some clothes and bumped my hair to meet Thomas in the reception area.

When I arrived, Dennis stood there holding the most gorgeous bouquet of hand-picked peonies in shades of pink. I was speechless, and impressed, and flattered—and despite my list I was about to go out with Dennis Oglesby. We went to Sonic and had cheeseburgers and fries along with hours of stimulating conversation. He was talented and witty. He was a member of the Omega Psi Phi fraternity and had recently been voted "Student of the Year."

But . . . he wasn't my type.

Although I began discreetly splitting my time between him and Thomas, they were exceedingly aware of each other. And I was having the time of my life. Twice a year, Rust would hold something called Open House. This was when the rules were relaxed, and a massive effort was undertaken that allowed both the men and women to fix up their quarters and see how the other half lived. So, I scrupulously cleaned and arranged my room. I was eager to have Thomas and Dennis survey my private domain first hand.

Thomas arrived at noon and was complementary about how I'd fashioned my small space. It was deliberately decorated with primary colors—the comforter, the rug, the accessories—and it was spotless. I, in turn, followed him to his room and was pleasantly surprised. It was neat and clean. And we laughed as he told me about how long it had taken him to get it to this state; if I opened his closet, he could officially be labeled a hoarder.

Careful not to have the two suitors overlap, I asked Dennis to arrive around 4:00 p.m. He walked in, and I could see him reverentially taking in my space. He commented on every detail—the vibrancy of the colors I chose and the position of the bed, the wall art and the family portraits on my desk. He even noticed the good luck charm Uncle Bud had given me, now hanging from my mirror. He then was a gracious host as he opened his small dwelling to my keen scrutiny. I had painted a mental picture of what I thought it would be like.

And when I saw it, I was spellbound by what I saw and in awe of the man who lived there. His room was sparsely furnished but attractive and inviting. His bed was clad in dark gray sheets and a matching comforter, tucked and folded military style. There was a leather club chair with a small side table. On that table was one of two retro lamps that warmly lit the room. He said he never used the overhead fluorescent lights. As I walked around taking in the sexiness of it all, I walked over to his desk. Strategically placed was a portfolio. I opened it and sat down in complete flummox by what lie inside: page after page of newspaper clippings of him singing the national anthem at White Sox games, facilitating workshops for the Chicago Urban league, volunteering for various nonprofit organizations, as well as his travels abroad. I was again rendered speechless.

I got back to my room that day and ceremoniously burned my list. In one afternoon I had come to realize that they were one-dimensional expectations that in no way dictated the measure of a man, nor should they come into play when seeking a meaningful relationship. I saw him with unsullied eyes that day. Here was a man who was well on his way to leaving his handprints on the world, and I wanted to be around to witness it.

CHAPTER FOURTEEN

Wedded Bliss

QUILT OF DREAMS

Wesley United Methodist Church was filled with 300 of our closest friends, family, and well-wishers. My wedding day was everything I dreamed it to be: A ceremony with singing, litanies, and vows we'd written to one another. Hazel was my matron of honor, and Sylvia and Yolanda were among fourteen bridesmaids wiping away tears as Daddy walked me down the aisle towards my destiny.

The reception was sumptuously catered by Aunt Tee, who had been sick of late, but maintained she was well enough to undertake such a taxing and extravagant event. She insisted it must be soul food. So, of course, there was fried chicken, potato salad, collard greens, and cornbread—and the most unbelievable wedding cake.

Aunt Tee was a hairdresser by trade, but she was also an extraordinary cake baker. It was exquisite. It rivaled anything we could have purchased from a bakery. There were three tiers of fifteen perfect cakes (buttercream cake with cream cheese frosting) that gracefully got smaller as each tier spiraled higher. The two side tiers were connected to the center tier by little golden stairs. On the left set of stairs were little groomsmen, and on the right were little bridesmaids, all appearing to be in procession. And at the top, of course, were a miniature bride and groom. Aunt Tee had carefully hand painted the tiny attendants brown. And at the proper time during the reception, the little stairs lit up. Oh . . . it was quite the conversation piece.

Mama and Daddy were so proud. I had gone away to school and met the man of my dreams, graduated that spring and, with the blessing of my father, was now being given to him in marriage. I couldn't wait to start my life with him. He was everything I wanted in a man, but just as importantly, he had won the respect of my father.

A week before the nuptials, Hazel threw a wedding shower for me. The room was overflowing with everything bridal—lots of tulle and white flowers, candles and gifts. It was mid-July, and each woman wore her favorite summer hat. As each individual guest was announced, the women oohed and ahhed over her hat choice. I was showered with sheets and towels, lingerie and a few other naughty things.

As the evening began to wind down, my brothers Shane and Ray brought in a final gift and set it at my feet. It was fairly large, wrapped in a sheet, and tied with a silver ribbon. I anxiously unwrapped the gift and, as the sheet fell away, I was taken aback at what lay beneath. Fat tears fell from my eyes and stung my cheeks as the old hope chest was revealed. I looked up at Mama. "How? Where has it been? How did you . . ."

"Unbeknownst to your Aunt Sadie, Big Otha confiscated it before they separated. When Big Otha finally died, Gilbert Earl didn't want it and gave it to CeCe. A few years ago CeCe gave it to me, said she wanted you to have it on your wedding day."

As the women held their collective breath, I opened it and carefully lifted each precious gift from the old heirloom. Mama had stored away some beautiful things for me: thirsty white towels and sheets made of pure cotton, airy sleeping gowns and house shoes, the Holy Bible, and at the bottom peeking through a layer of thin tissue paper was a quilt in the palest of blues. It was Mama's quilt she had received from her mother on the eve of her wedding.

The very sight of it took my breath away. I removed the precious endowment from its resting place. The women eagerly cleared a path for me, creating a make-shift aisle as I elegantly wrapped myself in the quilt and promenaded through the guests like a bride on her wedding day, a queen before her court. The women encircled me and blessed me with words of wisdom, and the evening ended with a prayer.

Dennis had accepted an administrative position at our alma mater. So, upon returning from our Caribbean honeymoon, we were heading back to Mississippi. Daddy helped us pack the last of the wedding gifts that had been stored at their house in the back of the rental car. Mama hated sad goodbyes, so we hugged and kissed inside. I hugged and kissed my father at the curb and slipped into my side of the car. I watched the two most important men in my life exchange a firm handshake and embrace one another in love. Then, in a broken voice, I heard my father say, "If somewhere down the road it doesn't work out, for whatever reason, you bring her back to me."

A sincere "Yes, sir" was the reply.

And with that, Daddy walked back to the house and stood in the doorway. I didn't want to pull off until he went inside. But he just stood there. I was fine until that moment, and I began to sob, "Wave to him, honey. Wave to him so he'll go inside." We waved and he waved back, but he didn't budge. Finally I said, "Just pull off, honey, just go." It would be many years later that my father told me he couldn't go inside until the tears stopped flowing. He didn't want Mama to see him cry.

Mama said there'd be days like this. She said having a baby was no laughing matter. She said if you think about the most excruciating pain you've ever felt in your life, it's ten times worse than that. She'd always say, "Baby, they tell me you pass Death nine times while you're on that delivery table." And as agonizing as my labor was, I believe I shook Death's hand at least eight times. But Mama also said that once that little gift arrived and I kissed its little face and touched its little fingers and toes, I would feel a love like I'd never known. And she was right. When that little six-pound girl arrived, it was simply the purest form of love I'd ever felt in my life. I wanted to do everything for her and be the best mother I could possibly be. And to see Dennis hold her in his arms just melted my heart. The nurses kept commenting on how beautiful she was and that she was the quietest newborn in the nursery.

Meghann Dominique was the best baby—until we got her home. She cried for hours on end. I thought I was losing my mind. We found that riding her around in the car somehow soothed her. So, we took turns, daily traversing the winding roads of Marshall County to lull our little angel to sleep. Mama arrived a week later, to help bring a sense of normalcy to our lives. Her eyes glistened with tears as she held Meg for the first time. She kissed each one of her tiny toes and promptly nicknamed her "Sugarfoot." And she began to lavish us all with love. She cooked salmon croquettes with eggs and buttered rice every morning. And she had a way of rocking Meghann that put her right to sleep.

When Meg turned a year old, we decided to move back to Chicago. I landed a job as an accountant for the City of Chicago's Department of Sewers while Dennis finished out his contract with Rust College.

I couldn't have asked for a better babysitter than Aunt Sky. She fell in love with Miss Meghann. My little angel walked around with a bit of an attitude, and Aunt Sky loved the ground she walked on. In her eyes, Meg could do no wrong. After six months, Dennis joined us, and we moved to an apartment on 12th and Michigan, making our home on the twenty-eighth floor.

I was just getting in from work and stopped at the grocery store on the lower level. On my way up to the apartment, the elevator stopped on the first floor. The doors opened to a well-dressed woman in a wheel chair. She rolled in and positioned herself beside me with effortless precision.

"What floor would you like?" I asked.

"Two please," she said, removing her sunglasses. "Greta, is that you?"

I was totally taken aback. "CeCe! I didn't recognize you!"

By this time, we had bypassed two and were on our way to the twenty-eighth floor. I invited her in and offered her something to drink.

"What happened? How did you end up like this?"

She sipped her soda and began telling me about her ordeal. "Well, about a year ago, I was on the bus minding my own business, and these two guys started in with me. I thought to myself, 'Oh my God, here we go.' Now, you know me. I've never been one to back down from nothin'. I've always had to take up for myself. They wouldn't let up, so I dropped my CeCe voice and started talkin' in my Otha voice. Girl, that pissed them off. The short, fat one pulled out a gun and shot me. The bullet lodged in my spine, and I've been paralyzed ever since."

We had been talking about forty-five minutes when Dennis arrived home with Meg. He was visibly shocked by what he walked in on.

"Babe, this is CeCe." There was an awkward silence. "Remember I told you about CeCe, the one who gave us the hope chest?"

He still wasn't connecting the dots. Finally CeCe said, "Let me get on home. Greta, it's so good to see you, girl. It's nice to meet you, Dennis. He blew Meg a kiss and said, "I'm in 208. Don't y'all be strangers."

The next several years seemed to fly by with lightening speed. Four years later I was pregnant with another baby. CeCe had been moved to a nursing home the year before because she could no longer care for herself. Dennis was working as a consultant for the Chicago Housing Authority. He also had been called to the ministry. So, he was enrolled at Northwestern, getting a master of divinity degree while serving as pastor of a small church in suburban Evanston.

With a new baby on the way, we needed more space. We settled on a house on South Vernon. It was an old antebellum that needed a lot of work. Dennis wasn't sold right away, but I saw its potential the minute I laid eyes on it. I told Daddy my vision, and he and Chappy Smith went to work. They gutted it, knocked out walls, raised the floor in the dining room, expanded the kitchen, and put in new tiles, appliances, and a center island. We installed new siding, with a double porch on the front and a huge deck on the back. It took about six months from start to finish. And the transformation was magnificent! We were simply house proud.

I was due to give birth any day, so we gave the house warming and baby shower simultaneously. A week later, Chase Michael arrived weighing seven pounds, five ounces. His was such a long, difficult birth. Dennis said (and we laugh about it now) that in my agony, not only did I speak in tongues, but I pulled my doctor to me and said, "Tie my tubes now!" But Chase was such a good baby. While Meghann had been a screamer, Chase was quiet as a mouse— sometimes so quiet I'd check on him just to make sure he was OK.

I had a couple of weeks of recuperation and was ready to show him to the world. After leaving our church in Evanston that Sunday, I took him by Daddy's church to show him off there. The benediction was just being given, so I slipped into a back pew until it was over. Tobby spotted us when the prayer ended and enthusiastically made his way to us. Soon, there was a throng of people around us, just trying to get a first look. In the midst of all the celebration, Daddy said into the microphone, "Someone call an ambulance." There was a stunned silence. And then he said, "We need an ambulance now!"

There was a leap to action. Tobby ran to call the paramedics, and a mass was now gathering around the pulpit. I held Chase close and made my way through the crowd. Aunt Sky was sitting in the middle of the mass of people, propped up by pillows. She was having trouble catching her breath. She pulled out her inhaler and took in two shallow breaths. Over the next several minutes her condition rapidly deteriorated. By the time the paramedics arrived, she was unconscious.

They were able to revive her, but only to a comatose state. She had suffered a massive stroke. The days and weeks went by, and there was no sign that she would awake from the deep slumber. Her daughter Sharon was always there to make sure her hair was combed and her favorite gospel music was playing. I hated going to that hospital. It sickened me to see her in that condition, machines and tubes keeping her alive. I can still remember the smell that permeated the halls of St. Bernard Hospital—a mixture of alcohol, penicillin, and slow death. The ICU was filled with patients who were in the last stages of life.

Over the next month, Aunt Sky, our bright light, dimmed right before our eyes. And on a clear, sunny morning in October, she danced off to glory, surrounded by those who loved her. And her beloved gospel music playing in the background was like a grand orchestra accompanying her as she crossed over to the other side.

The downtown office of the Department of Sewers was hectic, grueling, and teeming with people wanting to know why their water had been shut off in the dead of winter. Flow charts and cost reports were never-ending. But I loved it. I had always been fascinated with numbers, so, working in Chicago's City Hall as an accountant was a dream come true. My co workers and I were a tight-knit family unit, and my boss was like a guru we all respected and looked up to. And he always rewarded us for a job well done with drinks on Fridays at lunch and again at happy hour. We were in the midst of the annual budget crunch, when the profit and loss statement had to be accurate and the bottom line numbers on the balance sheet had to match. I was taking a much-needed coffee break in my office and flipping through the *Chicago Sun-Times* when I ran across an audition notice:

> The Chicago Theatre Company is looking for 6 African-American women who can sing Gospel for "Mens" the musical. Please prepare a 2-minute monologue and a song. Please call the theatre between 10 a.m. and 3 p.m. to schedule an audition time.

I thought to myself: I'm African-American. I sing Gospel. I should go out for this audition. It could be fun. It would certainly be a little extra money. I had never heard of this theater before, and it was literally blocks from my house. So, my mind was made up. I was throwing caution to the wind, and I was going. I had none of the things you need as an actor: no head shot, no resume, no monologue. The only thing I had was a song.

On the day of the audition, I left City Hall and headed to the library and committed to memory a little poem by Langston Hughes. It was all of thirty seconds long. But I kept telling myself: Talk slowly. S-t-r-e-t-c-h i-t o-u-t. Make it seem like it's longer than it really is. When I arrived at the theater, there had to be a hundred Black women there vying for these six roles. I was a fish out of water. I was totally out of my element. Every woman that arrived was greeted with hugs and a proverbial camaraderie. Why did they all know each other? What the hell was I doing? The voice in my right ear whispered: "You don't belong here. Leave before it's too late, before you make a fool of yourself." But I could hear Daddy's voice in my left ear reassuring me: "You can do it. . . . Face your fears. . . . Climb that mountain."

When the stage manager called my name I was literally shaking, but I wasn't about to let that nagging voice in my right ear talk me out of one of these roles. I followed her downstairs to the ninety-nine-seat theater, greeted the director, and started with my monologue—which sucked to high heaven.

"Uh, thank you, Ms. Oglesby," scoffed the director. It was clear she had heard enough. "Uh, have you prepared a song?

I nodded yes and immediately began an a cappella version of the hymn, "Great Is Thy Faithfulness." I had only sung in church and had developed a horrible habit of closing my eyes when I sang. I justified the bad practice by telling myself, "I'm not singing to man; I'm singing to God." When I finished my song and opened my eyes, a number of people, including the artistic director, had come out of their offices, inspired I guess by my rendition of this simple hymn.

"Where's your head shot and resume?" asked the artistic director.

"I'm sorry, I don't have either. This is my first audition."

He quickly took an instant Polaroid of me and attached it to the information sheet I'd filled out. I got a call back. And a week later, I got the part. Here I was working as an accountant for the city of Chicago, living my dream—or so I thought—and I stumble into acting, completely fall in love with it, and find it is something that I absolutely cannot live without.

That theater experience opened something in me that I never even knew was there. It's as though . . . I came into myself. Opening night of that little musical would mark a significant defining moment that would change the direction of the rest of my life. I knew beyond a shadow of a doubt that I wanted to dedicate my life to the mission of inspiring others.

CHAPTER FIFTEEN

Gossip & Biscuits

LIFE & LAUGHTER

As the years rolled by, Mama and I became friends, good friends. It wasn't until after I turned thirty that I found myself totally treasuring the time I spent with her. She fed me intellectually, emotionally, spiritually, and, oh my God, she made me laugh. She had the most wonderful way of being obliviously funny.

After the birth of my second child, my body clock changed and will forever be set at 6:00 a.m. Most every Saturday morning Mama would call around 6:30 a.m., "Hey, Girl, where should we go this mornin'?" We'd toss around a few possibilities, but would usually end up at Gladys' Luncheonette on 45th and King Drive. Gladys' had the best biscuits this side of heaven. Sometimes we'd get there and they'd be out of biscuits. But we'd sit and talk and drink coffee until a hot batch came up, because just the biscuits alone were worth the wait. And the conversation was always enlivening. We would recap the week's events from the church, to neighbors, to work.

One morning our breakfast conversation went like this: "You remember Mavis Gray? She's the teacher in the room across the hall from me. About a month ago she comes to me with a sad story and needs to borrow $20 until payday. Now, I go in my purse, into my bill money, to loan this woman this money. Honey, I want you to know payday came, and that woman walked all over and around me like she didn't even know me. Oooh, I was out-done. But I kept my mouth shut. The next payday came and went, and the woman still hadn't said two words to me about my $20. So by now it's not about the money, it's about the principle and her word. Baeeeeby, when that third payday came, and Mavis walked past me going into her classroom—Greta, it seemed like somethin' stood up in me."

By this time we are turning Gladys' out! I have fallen over laughing in the booth across from Mama. I am laughing hysterically because I'm picturing Mama, who is soft-spoken and non-confrontational, serve this woman notice!

"Greta, I opened the door to Room 201 so hard it hit the wall and chipped the plaster on impact. She stood up slowly with a look on her face like she wanted to run, but the only way out was the door I was standing in. I walked up to her, looked her dead in the eye, with my hand outstretched, and said, 'I come for my package.' Honnney, you should have seen Miss Mavis fallin' all over herself and apologizing as she rushed to her purse to get my money."

We sat in Gladys' a long time that day and laughed about Mavis and that $20. Like Aunt Sky would say, "Baeeeby, we sat up in there and shook a while."

The call came that Thursday morning that CeCe had died in her sleep. I remember thinking, "How like CeCe—to just sleep away." I hadn't seen her in months. And I felt bad that so much time had gone by and we'd fallen out of touch. But I would be at the memorial to see her one last time. She hadn't been an active member of a church, so Gilbert Earl arranged for her home going to take place at one of Chicago's most prestigious crematories. A torrent of scandalous talk began snaking its way through the family, because none of our relatives had ever been cremated. They believed a dirt burial was the most sacred way.

The viewing was set for the following Monday at 11:00 a.m., with the service to follow promptly at noon. I had taken off from work that day. When I arrived at 11:45, there were only a handful of mourners in attendance. Where were family members? Where was Gilbert Earl? The name at the entrance to the chapel read

"Otha Simmons Jr. I walked up the center aisle and rested my coat and purse on a seat in the second row. As I slowly approached the casket, I was completely stunned at what my eyes began to take in. It wasn't CeCe at all. It was Otha. Literally. He was dressed in a grey suit with a lavender shirt and a grey and white striped tie. His hair was cut neat and low. And the beard on his face had been groomed and chiseled by a master barber. Otha had lived most of his life as a woman who took great pride in flawless makeup, the right wig, and the perfect little dress. But stretched out in this fine silver coffin lay the body of a handsome man, a man I didn't know. And as I stood there in awe, I couldn't help but notice the slightest wrinkle in his brow. I'm sure CeCe was pissed! How could Gilbert Earl lay her out in such a way? Otha had been CeCe for more than thirty years, and CeCe is who we were coming to pay final respects to. Did Gilbert Earl hate CeCe that much, loathe her lifestyle so much, that he couldn't even allow her final bow on life's stage to be authentically hers? To take that from her and disregard her life in such a way made me so incredibly sad. I gathered my things and headed back to work.

Hazel called to say she had been there, as were other family members, but were utterly disheartened by what they'd encountered and immediately left. She said she saw Gilbert Earl and asked him why. He unequivocally declared, "I wasn't gone stretch out no drag queen for people to parade in here to see. He was born a man, and I feel it's only proper that he leave here a man." How unfair life could be sometimes. I just hoped that wherever CeCe was, she was happy and dressed to the nines!

Mama was my runnin' buddy. We'd dine together, go shopping together, and many times run errands together. This particular Saturday, my children wanted to go to the mall. (Meg was eight and Chase was four.) We picked Mama up around noon and first headed for Old Country Buffet. We were last in the uncommonly long line. It took thirty minutes just to reserve a table. When we reached the register to place our order, I was momentarily speechless. At once

I was cold and hot at the same time. I could feel thousands of tiny prickles in my armpits as my knees buckled ever so slightly. There she was, even taller than I remembered. But the face was exactly the same.

"May I help you?" she asked politely.

"Uh . . . four . . . for lunch," I spluttered.

"That will be $24.98," she said courteously.

I rifled clumsily through my purse and extracted $30.00. I cautiously handed her the money, careful only to look at her eyes when they weren't looking at me. I was riveted. Was it really her? Was I mistaken?

She skillfully retrieved my change from the register drawer and handed it to me. As her gaze met mine, I was flabbergasted. "Would you like something else?" she asked.

Several moments would go by before I was able to ask the question, "Is your name Lorena Salter?"

"Salter was my maiden name," she said, completely perplexed. "Now it's Henderson."

"Well, my name is Greta Lacy. Do you remember me?"

"No," she said.

"Do I look familiar at all?"

"No," she repeated.

I hastily began to narrate the details of our brief grade school history: "We attended fifth grade together. It was Bass Elementary School. Mrs. Jackson was the teacher."

She nodded her head yes in affirmation.

"Remember the mobile units?"

"Oh, my God. Yes!" She exclaimed.

"Well," I continued, "do you remember you and Connie Williamson ran me home every single day for about a month before I transferred?" I began to recount specific incidents.

She shook her head in disbelief. She didn't remember me at all, or Connie Williamson, or any of the harrying episodes. She was genuine in her incredulity, stating she had been through a horrible bullying experience with one of her own daughters, and that she wouldn't wish it on her worst enemy. She truly didn't remember but gave me the most sincere apology. And I wholeheartedly accepted.

We dined sufficiently at Old Country Buffet that day, with Mama recalling parables regarding "reaping what you sow," and lessons about "what goes around comes around."

After lunch, we said goodbye to Lorena and set out for the Algonquin Mills Mall, about a forty-minute drive. As soon as we got on the highway, Chase (who has a fixation with public restrooms) said, "Mommy, I have to use it," exclaiming he had to do number two. (Mind you, he'd already used it at Old Country Buffet.)

So, I was not moved because this was all so familiar to me. I told him, "No, you'll have to hold it until we get to the mall."

But he whined until he had Mama convinced and at her wits end. She offered him candy, money, trips to the park and zoo. But he was having none of it. Chase was a child who just wanted to have his way. And he'd whine until you were so irritated, you'd just give in to stop the madness.

He carried on for about twenty minutes. And Mama was fresh out of bribes. She was so frustrated, she finally pleaded with him, "Baby, please try to hold it until we get to the mall. It won't be much longer." And as she literally looked around the floor of the car, she said in all sincerity, "Because we don't have a bucket or even a big jar in the car right now." I just shook my head and chuckled to myself because as peculiar as that statement was, and the visual of it, it was so innately normal to Mama.

I had breakfast at Gladys' with my sister Hazel the next day. And as we buttered our hot biscuits, I told her about the Lorena Salter encounter, and we hollered awhile about Mama, the bucket, and the jar.

CHAPTER SIXTEEN

Altar Call

& A KNIGHT IN SHINING ARMOR

Now, on Saturdays, Aunt Tee's kitchen was no longer the gathering place to get our hair done and to fellowship. Something in the universe had shifted. Her good health began to fail. And she was very private about her condition. Sometimes Uncle Ira had to help her get up and down the stairs because her legs had grown very weak. After her eyesight began to fail, he told us she had diabetes.

One day he came home from work to find Aunt Tee on the floor. She was sprawled out on the landing by the front door. Her health had declined over the last few years, and Edwin's behavior was becoming increasingly more erratic. Initially, he was labeled as developmentally disabled, but had recently been diagnosed as also having schizophrenia. He had rigged a piece of string across the bottom three stairs. Aunt Tee left her bedroom and was on her way to the kitchen. He watched her feel her way along the hallway and down the stairs, then trip over the string. His antics were no longer mischievous, but mean-spirited. Uncle Ira packed Edwin's bags and had the Department of Children and Family Services pick him up and take him away. Aunt Tee was heartbroken, but she knew he had to go.

After a time, she was only able to see shadows and eventually succumbed to a wheelchair. But Uncle Ira brought her to church every Sunday as she requested. She couldn't see or walk, but she made sure he still took food to those who were hungry and money to those in need. And through it all, she still gave thanks to the Lord. She'd say, "If the Lord don't heal me, it ain't because he can't." She believed her healing was just a prayer away, that it was just a matter of time.

Now, Reverend James came every year to preach the closing sermon for Daddy's annual Pastor's Anniversary celebration. On this day, all monies raised would go to Daddy in appreciation for another year of service. And every year, when raising this offering, Reverend James would pompously announce, "Now, beloveds, those of you who are able, I want you to follow my lead as I start this offering with $100." And every year, without fail, when the deacons counted the money, Reverend James's envelope would be audaciously empty.

Reverend James also boasted of being a healer. He said he could lay hands on the sick and make them well, that just the touch of his hand could make blinded eyes see. And Aunt Tee was both. Just before the close of this service, Reverend James made an altar call, but he only called one person down front: Aunt Tee. He said, "Now, beloveds, you are going to witness a miracle here today. In this very room a miracle is about to take place."

Then he spoke directly to Aunt Tee. "Now, Sister Johnson, not only have you been sick in your body, but it's been a long time since you've seen your husband's face. But, dear heart, today all that's about to change." As he beckoned an usher to roll her wheelchair down to the altar, Aunt Tee began to weep and shout praises to God.

There was a stirring in the congregation. Everything about this felt wrong. Something started turning in the pit of my stomach. Who was he to make such claims? A man who was known to have extra-marital affairs, who cheated and deceived when he thought no one was looking? Why would God bestow such an extraordinary gift on such a carnal human being? I wanted someone to stop him; no good could come of this. But no one spoke out. No one said a word.

The usher rolled her down and locked the wheelchair in place. "Now, dear heart, do you want your eyesight restored today?"

Aunt Tee shouted, "Yes!"

He told her to close her eyes and said, "Sister, prepare to receive your miracle." He took the white handkerchief he was holding, put a little spit on it, carefully rubbed each of her eyes, and then said a prayer. When he finished, there was a profound hush. I think people had unconsciously stopped breathing awaiting the outcome. He waved the open hanky in front of her face and shouted, "Now, open your eyes!" She did so ever so slowly, as we all watched in absolute silence. He said, "Sister, can you see?"

After about thirty seconds, she shook her head and quietly said, "No, sir." There were gasps all over the church.

"Lord, have mercy," escaped from someone's lips.

He then shouted, "Shut your eyes again, Mother!" She did so. This time he put a little spit on the handkerchief and covered her entire head with it. He prayed again fervently and asked us all to stretch our right hands in Aunt Tee's direction.

He then removed the hanky and admonished her again, "Mother, open your eyes and tell me, can you see?"

A single tear rolled down her cheek, as she shook her head no.

Embarrassed, he immediately said, "Of course you can't see, because God works in mysterious ways and according to your belief."

I was aghast. How dare he be so arrogant! So thoughtless! The entire church surrounded her and tried to give her words of encouragement as the service was brought to a close. We all believed in the power of prayer and healing. Unfortunately, Reverend James was not the vessel God would use to bring that healing about.

During Aunt Tee's final months, she said she saw spirits. And I truly believe she did. And when she'd see them, she'd call them out, she'd talk to them, "Hey, get your vile self from around here! I see you! You have no place here! Git! Git outta here!" Throughout her long illness, Uncle Ira was there—faithful, loving, and devoted. He cooked for her, bathed her, dressed her, and paid every hospital bill.

On a Sunday morning, Aunt Tee passed quietly in her sleep. She had made all her final arrangements before her passing. And it was a funeral fit for a queen. The church was overflowing. Choirs sang, countless resolutions were read, and the pastor preached her right into the bosom of Jesus. She was simply divine as she lay there with those smiling eyes and her long black curls framing her little round face. She wore white. And Uncle Ira made sure she was wrapped in her favorite mink stole.

Later, at the cemetery, just as they began to lower her into the ground, with one hand Uncle Ira used his knuckles and made two quick taps on the top of her casket. Mama said she thought it was his way of telling her he would be joining her soon. I didn't know what it meant, but I had found deep respect for this man with the stone face. He had been there for her in every conceivable way. He had been her knight in shining armor. And he had truly loved her in sickness and in health 'til death they did part.

CHAPTER SEVENTEEN

Flights of Angels

ALLELUIA AMEN

As Mama got older and somewhat feeble, she would share information with me that I was to hold in strict confidence. I knew it was hush-hush because, just as she was about to share this covert information, she would look over both shoulders to ensure no one was listening and quietly preface her comment with, "Now, between you and me . . ." Now, the top secret discussion was never a secret because Mama would whisper the clandestine information to each of my siblings in the exact same manner. So, the would-be undisclosed conversation was always public knowledge amongst the family.

She wasn't getting around too well these days. Like Aunt Tee, Mama had been diagnosed with diabetes, and it was beginning to take its toll. She would sit in her favorite chair in front of the TV and watch the morning news, an occasional game show, and her soap operas. She affectionately called them "my stories." So, we'd take turns helping around the house and running errands for her.

It was a Saturday, and I had come by with some specific items she wanted from the store. I put the groceries away, fixed her a light lunch, and started cleaning, when she called me over to her, "Greta, come here a minute." She looked over both her shoulders and whispered, "Now, between you and me . . ."

I stifled the laugh rising in my belly, but I couldn't hide the smile forming in the corners of my mouth. Before she continued, she turned the volume down on the TV, looked me square in the eye, and whispered, "I got a letter from Ed McMahon. It was addressed directly to me, says he thinks I might be the winner of ten million dollars."

For a few moments I was bemused. And as I sat there contemplating a response, what happened next foretold the magnitude of what would take place over the next several weeks. Mama pulled out four letters from her purse, all from Publisher's Clearing House. On the back of each letter was a picture of Ed McMahon with that famous smile and his handsome, computer-generated signature. She had responded to each letter by ordering some magazines, and a subsequent letter would arrive saying she was closer to becoming the ten million dollar winner. When I spoke to Hazel that night, of course she and my other siblings already knew about the confidential letters from Ed McMahon, so, we planned an intervention for the following weekend.

That Saturday, Daddy had prepared a bountiful breakfast as we all pulled our chairs up to the family dining table. A conversation that started out light and loving quickly took an eerie turn. We were lovingly trying to convince Mama that she had not been singled out by Mr. McMahon, but that millions of other people were receiving the same letters. But there was no dissuading her. It all seemed so absurd. She wasn't thinking clearly. She felt as though we were conspiring against her in some way. She said, "If y'all don't want to be a part of my ten million dollar windfall, then I will just reap all the benefits myself."

Over the next several weeks, letters regularly came from Publisher's Clearing House with tidbits of information about the upcoming date announcing the ten million dollar winner. The correspondence always pitched their magazines, while appearing to speak personally to Mama as the potential winner. Inevitably, a final letter came. It told her the date they would announce the winner. It further said that potential winners should not leave their homes that day, to watch for the famous Publisher's Clearing House van and to watch their televisions for the big reveal.

The day arrived, and we were all assembled at Mama's. We couldn't let her go through this alone. There was a sickness in the pit of my stomach and an aching around my heart. It was utter torture. It was excruciating, waiting and watching for a van we knew ultimately would never come. And at 4:00 p.m. the inevitable happened. We all watched the television in silence as the white van pulled up in front of a modest-looking brick home. The spirited announcer got out of the van along with a team of cheerful assistants carrying balloons. An elderly white woman answered the door and began to cry. She held up the over-sized ten million dollar check and was clearly overwhelmed by it all. And just like that, it was over, done. And the regular programming resumed.

We sat in Mama's living room in silence for what seemed like hours, each of us desperately trying to form expressions of consolation, but no words would come. There was nothing to say that would make this better. I don't know what Mama was feeling or what was going through her mind, but the look on her face made me feel a sadness I'd never felt before and I've never felt since. Finally, Daddy came in with some food. He didn't ask about the outcome of the Publisher's Clearing House Sweepstakes; he knew. He lovingly kissed Mama's forehead and began to set the table for us all to eat.

Mama was the best kind of nurturer. She loved each one of us individually and unconditionally. She had taken such good care of us all, not out of obligation but because she delighted in it. She did most of the cooking and cleaning, and whenever Daddy sat down to a meal she always fixed his plate. It was her good pleasure to do so. Daddy counted on her to see to our needs, run the household, and take care of the finances. She was also his right hand at the church. She visited the sick and shut in, lead prayer meetings, and sat on the Mother's Board. And every chicken dinner ever made to raise money for the church, Mama had a hand in it. Daddy was a man's man. He had vigor and stamina and the strength of a bull in his arms. It seemed he could do anything. He painted, welded, fixed cars, our bikes, the plumbing, the roof, and the furnace.

I remember one winter our gas was turned off. Daddy cut a hole in the wall near the kitchen and installed a wood burning stove to heat the house. (Wherever we went, our clothes always reeked of smoke, but we had heat.) Once on a trip to the grocery store, with my kids in the back seat, I ran over a huge pothole in the street. The impact was so jarring Meghann exclaimed, "Mommy, we have to get Granddad to fix these awful potholes!" He was the man who did it all. Even my kids thought Daddy was invincible and could take care of everything.

But with all his knowledge of fixing and taking care of things, he didn't know how to take care of Mama when she got sick. Out of all the things he knew how to do, he didn't know how to nurture. Mama was in the final season of her sojourn, and she now needed him to take care of her. Now when I visited her, I could still sense the angels about her, but they were now hovering for a different reason.

Daddy was now retired, but began taking odd jobs doing carpentry and plumbing. Sometimes he'd be gone for hours, rendering her helpless to get food or relieve herself. One day my brother Shane stopped by the house to check on Mama and found her on the kitchen floor. She had fallen out of her wheelchair trying to get something to eat. Daddy had been gone since the morning, and it was well past midday. She had been lying there helpless for more than an hour. Shane was livid. He gathered her up and set her back in her chair. She wasn't hurt, thank God, but she was hungry. She eagerly ate the sandwich he prepared, but when he asked if she needed to go to the bathroom, she insisted on waiting for Daddy. She was comfortable only with him helping her with her most private matters.

Just as Shane cleared away the dishes, Daddy walked in with two Styrofoam containers filled with piping hot food from the corner diner. Instinctively he knew he was too late. When Shane beckoned Daddy outside, he could feel the rage twitching underneath his skin.

He called me that evening with his searing words to my father: "I'm gone say this once, and I'm never gone say it again. If I ever come by here and find Mama hungry, thirsty, unclean, in need of relieving herself, or in need of anything that is completely in your capability to do, God help you, 'cause you gone have to answer to me." He didn't have to say anything more, the look in Shane's eyes said it all. The two men came to an understanding that day. What seemed like a threat was really a covenant sealed between them.

Two years after Mama died, Daddy finally felt ready to part with her things. He told us all to come by and select what we wanted. I told him I'd be by after work about 4:00. Just as I was about to hang up, he said it: "I love you." I was thunderstruck and completely overcome with emotion. I couldn't even say it back to him! The lump in my throat was strangling me, and the torrent of tears soaked the papers on my desk. I closed the door to my office, not only to gather myself, but to savor the moment. He said it. I couldn't believe he finally said it. It was so long in coming, I didn't even know how to receive it.

When I got to the house, he hugged me long and hard, then directed me to the master bedroom. Daddy had laid her things out on their king-sized bed. As I ran my hand over each item, I vividly remembered her wearing each one of them. Some were sentimental pieces I would carefully wrap and store away, but others were heirlooms I would cherish and pass on to my daughter. There were exquisite hats she'd worn to church, coats she wore only for special occasions, and jewelry. But the item I treasure most is a cream and silver vintage shawl that adorns the chair beside my bed. I feel she is with me when I wake in the morning and when I slip into slumber at night.

Two weeks later, I visited Mama's grave for the first time. I was accompanied by Daddy and my brother Shane. A familiar winding road led us to the site. Actually, I had been here many times before, because also on this grassy hill lay Aunt Tee, Aunt Sky, Aunt Sadie, and Aunt Mae. During my visits I would smile as I thought of them individually and collectively, knowing how much of their handprints were on my life.

But this time it was all together different, all too surreal. Mama was here. As we approached her grave, I immediately missed her very presence, her touch, her smile, her laugh. And as I stood looking at her grave, I couldn't speak, my eyes watered incessantly, and there was a strange pull in the bottom of my stomach I couldn't explain. We didn't stay long; I found it all too overwhelming.

A year would go by before I got up enough courage to go back. This time I wanted to go alone. Whatever this visit would bring, I didn't want it to be a shared experience. I needed it to be my own.

It was a warm summer day as I rounded the familiar bend and could see the tranquil, grassy mound growing closer through the hazy sun. As I got out of my car and began approaching the place where she lay, fat tears came rushing back. As I stood over her grave, I could feel that strong pull in the bottom of my stomach, like a child attached to its mother by an umbilical cord.

There wasn't a soul in sight. So I slipped off my shoes and lay prostrate over her, sobbing salty tears into the warm grass. I called her name, "Mama. Mama. Mama." It felt so good, so cathartic. I lay there maybe fifteen minutes absorbing the sun and Mama. Oh . . . how I missed her . . . how I would never stop missing her. But somehow this simple, private, primal act was one of the most profound moments of clarity I have ever experienced.

After a while the tears stopped, and I was able to sit up. And I sat there for about an hour with the warm summer breeze washing over me, thinking of past, present, and future. It was a good visit. I left there that day truly with a light sense of being.

Chicago had been home to me all my life. I couldn't imagine living anywhere else. But when Dennis accepted the position of Minister to the City for a downtown church in Minneapolis, we wholeheartedly left Chicago to embark upon a new life in the Twin

Cities. Dennis had finished seminary and was living out his calling. I quit my "day job" of fourteen years and also began the passionate pursuit of my destiny.

"There are two women who say my words just like I hear them in my ear. You are one of them." Those were August Wilson's words to me at the opening of the world premier of *Gem of the Ocean* at the Goodman Theatre in Chicago in 2003. At the play's end, a deafening silence fell over the sold out house, followed by thunderous applause and a rousing standing ovation. *Gem of the Ocean* is Mr. Wilson's penultimate work in the epic ten-play cycle, The Wilson Cycle, which chronicles each decade of the African American experience in the twentieth century. *Gem* introduces us to Aunt Ester, the primal connection to the first slave ship from Africa, and the character that hovers over the entire Wilson cycle. So, when I received the call that Mr. Wilson wanted me to play the role of this incredible woman, Aunt Ester (an-cestor), I was ecstatic, deeply honored, and terrified. I was also humbled to know that he was entrusting me with this extraordinary role, trusting me to use my voice, my life experiences, and artistic process to create a template for whom and what Aunt Ester should be and ultimately became as the production premiered on Broadway in November 2004.

In Aunt Ester I see my mother, my grandmother, and all of my aunts. She is so familiar and familial to me. On Saturday's these women would convene in Aunt Tee's kitchen to get their hair done. And as a little girl, I sat at the feet of these women who imparted wisdom, grace, spirituality, wit, humor, virtue, and gave me the audacity to honor my own voice. I carry their spirits. August saw glimpses of those amazing women when he first saw me portray Bertha in Joe Turner's *Come and Gone* at Penumbra Theatre.

"It's all adventure. . . . you signed up for it and didn't even know it," Aunt Ester says in *Gem of the Ocean*. When I walked onto the stage of that little ninety-nine-seat theater, I had no idea what a magnificent adventure I was signing up for. For me, theatre is spiritual. It is a sanctuary, my calling. It is a matter of the heart. I will be eternally grateful to Mama 'n Nem for giving me a history that has shaped my destiny. I feel them sprinkling me with grace whenever I step into the sacred space of a theatre. And their spirits will always be like precious drops of water softly rippling throughout my life.

AFTERWORD

I am well into the fourth decade of my life, and I have never once found myself in search of myself. With all my schooling, there has been no greater education than the lessons I learned sitting at the feet of these ordinary yet extraordinary men and women—lessons that only knowledge and experience can bestow. They have always been, and continue to be, the symphony of my life. The faint echoes of their voices are like a cacophony of music rising and falling in syncopated rhythms, arias, movements, and beautiful harmonies. They will never know the impact of the precious life they poured into me. They were like wellsprings, truly rivers of living water that unendingly flow out of my belly and wash over me. They shaped me, layer upon layer of a tenderly evolving way of life. And their unquestionable love and guidance have given me the audacity to honor my own voice.

When I look at the trajectory of my own journey, I humbly like to think that I am somewhere in the middle of my life's arc, and each day Mama 'n Nem are yet guiding me. The oral history and spoken stories are parts of ancestry. That oral tradition is like a collection plate of our shared lives together. Priceless.

Growing up, Daddy embodied decency and goodness. It was a code he lived by. It was a standard of what I wanted my life to be. He never had a lot of money or material things to give us, but the life he lived before us was a light that always illumined a path for us, and whenever we veered off destiny's road that light was a beacon so we never lost our way. Someone once wrote, "I'd rather see a sermon than hear one." In my father I always saw a sermon—and what an eloquent one it was and, praise be to God, continues to be.

Mama was simply grace personified. She possessed a lifelong simplicity that I aspire to. She was like a beautiful tapestry hand-woven by God. She is my alma mater, that school of knowledge that I constantly reference when I hit a snag in the road of life.

I live each day with gratitude because there is a balance and emotional safety I possess because of them.

Their handprints mark my life.